JERKY

JERKY

13-Digit ISBN: 978-1-64643-217-2
10-Digit ISBN: 1-64643-217-7

This book may be ordered by mail from the publisher. Please include $5.99 for postage and handling. Please support your local bookseller first!

Books published by Cider Mill Press Book Publishers are available at special discounts for bulk purchases in the United States by corporations, institutions, and other organizations. For more information, please contact the publisher.

Cider Mill Press Book Publishers
"Where good books are ready for press"
501 Nelson Place
Nashville, Tennessee 37214

cidermillpress.com

Typography: Finland, Futura PT, Nobel, Quasimoda

Image Credits: Pages 13-14, 22-23, 34-35, 48-49, 59-60, 73, 74-75, 76, 79, 80-81, 88, 95-96, 98, 104-105, 108, 112, 112-113, 114, 116-117, 118, 122, 124-125, 127, 134-135, 137, 138-139, 144-145, 146, 155, 156-157, 159, 160, 162-163, 164, and 166-167 used under official license from Shutterstock.

All other photos courtesy of Keith Sarasin.

Printed in Malaysia

Back cover image: Honey & Jalapeño Pork Jerky, page 100
Back endpaper image: Hickory Beef Jerky, page 81

24 25 26 27 28 OFF 7 6 5 4 3

JERKY

THE ESSENTIAL COOKBOOK

70+
DELICIOUS
RECIPES

KEITH SARASIN

CIDER MILL PRESS
BOOK PUBLISHERS

For the Witham Family.

Thanks for the amazing love and family you have brought to my life over the last 10+ years.

To John for his amazing jerky skills, and for inspiring me to learn more about this art, thank you!

CONTENTS

INTRODUCTION

In a world that is increasingly on the go, one of its OG fast foods—jerky—has enjoyed a major renaissance these past few years, as people have rediscovered the convenience, versatility, and pragmatic potential that a strip of jerky carries.

The humble process of drying meat—trimming the fat from a piece of meat, cutting it into strips, salting them, and dehydrating them—has been around for millennia. One of the earliest forms of jerky, and the one that the word descends from, can be traced back to the Quechua people of South America, who dried llama and alpaca meat in the sun and then froze it during the cold nights that occur in the Andes Mountains. The foods preserved by these ingenious methods were known as ch'arki, which roughly translates into "to burn meat." Unlike the jerky we find today, records indicate that ch'arki was often dried on the bone.

Native Americans also had a version of jerky, known as pemmican. Pemmican was most often made by mixing ground-up venison with berries and fat and fashioning the mixture into a small cake that would then be smoked in order to preserve it. In addition to venison, fish and bison were also popular proteins used in pemmican.

These days, jerky is more than just dried meat. It comes in a variety of flavors that are supplied by various spice blends and marinades, as well as wood smoke. It is seen as a comfort food as much as a health food, with its high-protein, low-sugar composition making it appealing to those practicing the ketogenic diet and other low-carb approaches to eating.

BEST PRACTICES

As the Quechua demonstrated with their fondness for dehydrating alpaca and llama meat, just about any meat can be turned into jerky. But if you're enthusiastic enough about jerky to purchase a book about it, we're guessing that most of your excitement centers around beef jerky.

If that's the case, you'll want to focus your attention on these three cuts: eye round, bottom round, and top round. These have the lean character and low price tag you want when making jerky; filet mignon will also be lean, but it would be a mistake to make a habit of subjecting such a fine and pricey cut of meat to the withering ordeal of a lengthy stay in a dehydrator. The eye round is a single oval muscle found in the rear legs of a cow. As the grain runs the entire length of the cut, it's easy to cut against or with the grain. The bottom round is the outer muscles found in the upper rear legs of a cow. It has excellent flavor that, since it is relatively inexpensive, provides exceptional bang for the buck. The top round is similar to the bottom round, only it comes from the inner parts of the animal's rear legs.

Other cuts that work well for beef jerky are the sirloin tip and flank. Ground chuck can also provide good results, so long as you have a jerky gun (see the Tools section on page 12).

When using meats other than beef to make jerky, keep the same tenets in mind—lean and economical.

SAFETY FIRST

When working with meat, one must take the time and precautions to ensure that the process remains hygienic. When preserving meat, this becomes even more important. The following rules will keep you safe when making jerky, and guarantee the best results:

- Wash your hands before and after handling raw meat.
- Make sure you have a working surface that is clean and disinfected.
- Refrigerate raw meat at 40°F or below.
- If you are planning to use meat that is frozen, make sure to thaw the meat in the refrigerator, not on the kitchen counter.
- When marinating the meat, store it in the refrigerator. Do not reuse any marinade.
- If you are preparing jerky from wild game, make sure the hunter followed safe practices and that the animal was dressed properly.
- Let the meat come to a temperature of 160°F when drying it, as this will help decrease the possibility of bacterial growth.
- The thickness of the strips makes a difference. It is recommended not to slice the meat into strips any thicker than ¼ inch.
- Trim all the fat from the meat. It can become rancid and spoil the jerky.

If you follow these rules, you're well on your way to making quality jerky at home. Once these have become ingrained, the only real questions are what type of meat you want to use, and whether you want the jerky to be tender or chewy. If you want your jerky to have more chew, cut the meat with the grain, which is the direction that the muscle fibers are running in. For jerky that is toward the tender side, slice against the grain, which will shorten the muscle fibers and make it easier to chew. Should you find it a challenge to get the control you want when cutting meat into strips that have the proper thickness, place the meat in the freezer for 15 minutes before slicing it.

TOOLS

There are not a lot of materials required to make jerky—a well-stocked spice rack, an oven, and a few sheet pans will produce delicious results if one follows the instructions in this book. But should you want to get serious about your jerky making, there are a few items that are essential:

- **A good dehydrator.** One of my favorite dehydrators is the Excalibur 3926TB. This model has nine trays (so volume is not a problem), is incredibly efficient and easy to clean, and features a temperature range of 105°F to 165°F, meaning you can also use it to turn out fruit leather and vegetarian jerky.
- **A vacuum sealer.** Dehydrating meat will preserve it for a while, but if you're interested in really extending its shelf life, a good vacuum sealer is a must. Instead of a few weeks, your jerky will remain good for anywhere from 6 months to 2 years. FoodSaver offers a variety of quality models, and I use mine all the time.
- **A jerky gun or jerky cannon.** A must if you want to make jerky out of ground meat—and since it has an incredibly tender texture compared to regular jerky, I recommend giving it a try.
- **A meat thermometer.** This goes beyond making good jerky—it's a great investment for anyone who is serious about cooking and food safety. And remember, for jerky you want to bring the temperature of the meat to 160°F.
- **Kosher salt and curing salt.** The former will provide the flavor, and the latter will hinder bacterial growth and help prevent spoilage.

You're ready to start on your journey into the world of jerky. What's been discussed will help, I hope, but as with everything in the kitchen, going through the process on your own will serve as a far better teacher.

BEEF, PORK & POULTRY

As the display rack at every decent rest stop will attest, beef is the overwhelming favorite when it is time to choose a protein to make jerky. That is in large part due to how affordable and widely available it is, its generally lean character, and its ability to form pleasing partnerships with a number of different seasonings and flavor profiles.

This chapter does not cut against that tradition, with beef showing up in a bulk of the recipes. But the pork and poultry suggestions shouldn't be overlooked, providing a solid foundation that will quickly allow you to experiment with different seasoning blends and marinades.

TRADITIONAL BEEF JERKY

YIELD: 12 SERVINGS
ACTIVE TIME: 20 MINUTES
TOTAL TIME: 10½ TO 24 HOURS

The perfect recipe to get you started, providing a pleasant chew and a flavor that's agreeable to all.

INGREDIENTS

2 lbs. beef (top round or bottom round)

2 tablespoons brown sugar

2 tablespoons liquid smoke

¼ cup gluten-free tamari or soy sauce

1 teaspoon meat tenderizer

2 teaspoons kosher salt

1½ teaspoons black pepper

2 tablespoons Worcestershire sauce

2 teaspoons paprika

DIRECTIONS

1 Trim the meat to remove excess fat. Cut the meat into strips that are between ⅛ and ¼ inch thick, slicing with the grain for a chewier jerky or against the grain for a more tender jerky.

2 Place the remaining ingredients in a mixing bowl and whisk until the sugar has dissolved and the mixture is thoroughly combined.

3 Add the meat to the marinade and stir until the strips are evenly coated.

4 Cover the bowl with plastic wrap, place it in the refrigerator, and marinate for at least 6 hours. If time allows, let the meat marinate overnight.

5 Remove the meat from the refrigerator and give it a stir.

6 To prepare the jerky in a dehydrator, arrange the meat on the dehydrator trays, making sure to leave space between each piece. Place it in the dehydrator and dehydrate until the meat has dried out but is still flexible, 4 to 6 hours.

7 To prepare the jerky in an oven, preheat the oven to 175°F. Line two rimmed baking sheets with aluminum foil and place wire racks over the foil. Arrange the strips of meat on the racks, making sure to leave space between each piece and to keep the meat in a single layer. Place the pans in the oven and bake for 1½ hours. Rotate the pans and then bake until the meat is dry to the touch, leathery, and slightly chewy, 1½ to 2½ hours.

8 Store the jerky at room temperature in an airtight container, where it will keep for a few weeks. If you are interested in a longer shelf life for your jerky, place it in a bag and vacuum seal it. Stored in a cool, dry place, the vacuum-sealed jerky will keep for 6 months to 2 years.

EVERYTHING BAGEL BEEF JERKY

YIELD: 12 SERVINGS
ACTIVE TIME: 30 MINUTES
TOTAL TIME: 4½ TO 6½ HOURS

Everything bagel seasoning is increasingly available in grocery stores, but if you strike out at those nearby, head online.

INGREDIENTS

2 lbs. beef (top round or bottom round)

1 tablespoon brown sugar

1 teaspoon meat tenderizer

2 teaspoons kosher salt

1½ teaspoons black pepper

¼ cup everything bagel seasoning

DIRECTIONS

1. Trim the meat to remove excess fat. Cut the meat into strips that are between ⅛ and ¼ inch thick, slicing with the grain for a chewier jerky or against the grain for a more tender jerky.
2. Place the remaining ingredients in a mixing bowl and whisk until the mixture is thoroughly combined.
3. Add the meat to the rub and stir until the strips are evenly coated.
4. To prepare the jerky in a dehydrator, arrange the meat on the dehydrator trays, making sure to leave space between each piece. Place it in the dehydrator and dehydrate until the meat has dried out but is still flexible, 4 to 6 hours.
5. To prepare the jerky in an oven, preheat the oven to 175°F. Line two rimmed baking sheets with aluminum foil and place wire racks over the foil. Arrange the strips of meat on the racks, making sure to leave space between each piece and to keep the meat in a single layer. Place the pans in the oven and bake for 1½ hours. Rotate the pans and then bake until the meat is dry to the touch, leathery, and slightly chewy, 1½ to 2½ hours.
6. Store the jerky at room temperature in an airtight container, where it will keep for a few weeks. If you are interested in a longer shelf life for your jerky, place it in a bag and vacuum seal it. Stored in a cool, dry place, the vacuum-sealed jerky will keep for 6 months to 2 years.

SALT & VINEGAR BEEF JERKY

YIELD: 12 SERVINGS
ACTIVE TIME: 30 MINUTES
TOTAL TIME: 4½ TO 6½ HOURS

Using vinegar powder allows you to put this jerky directly in the dehydrator or oven.

INGREDIENTS

2 lbs. beef (tenderloin, top round, or bottom round)

1 tablespoon vinegar powder

1 teaspoon meat tenderizer

2½ teaspoons Maldon sea salt

DIRECTIONS

1. Trim the meat to remove excess fat. Cut the meat into strips that are between ⅛ and ¼ inch thick, slicing with the grain for a chewier jerky or against the grain for a more tender jerky.
2. Place the remaining ingredients in a mixing bowl and whisk until the mixture is thoroughly combined.
3. Add the meat to the rub and stir until the strips are evenly coated.
4. To prepare the jerky in a dehydrator, arrange the meat on the dehydrator trays, making sure to leave space between each piece. Place it in the dehydrator and dehydrate until the meat has dried out but is still flexible, 4 to 6 hours.
5. To prepare the jerky in an oven, preheat the oven to 175°F. Line two rimmed baking sheets with aluminum foil and place wire racks over the foil. Arrange the strips of meat on the racks, making sure to leave space between each piece and to keep the meat in a single layer. Place the pans in the oven and bake for 1½ hours. Rotate the pans and then bake until the meat is dry to the touch, leathery, and slightly chewy, 1½ to 2½ hours.
6. Store the jerky at room temperature in an airtight container, where it will keep for a few weeks. If you are interested in a longer shelf life for your jerky, place it in a bag and vacuum seal it. Stored in a cool, dry place, the vacuum-sealed jerky will keep for 6 months to 2 years.

SPICY BBQ BEEF JERKY

YIELD: 12 SERVINGS
ACTIVE TIME: 30 MINUTES
TOTAL TIME: 10½ TO 24 HOURS

Don't hesitate to experiment with the level of heat here, as well as different chili powders.

INGREDIENTS

2 lbs. beef (top round or bottom round)

1 tablespoon brown sugar

1 teaspoon meat tenderizer

2 teaspoons kosher salt

1½ teaspoons black pepper

½ cup barbecue sauce

2 tablespoons chili powder

DIRECTIONS

1. Trim the meat to remove excess fat. Cut the meat into strips that are between ⅛ and ¼ inch thick, slicing with the grain for a chewier jerky or against the grain for a more tender jerky.
2. Place the remaining ingredients in a mixing bowl and whisk until the sugar has dissolved and the mixture is thoroughly combined.
3. Add the meat to the marinade and stir until the strips are evenly coated.
4. Cover the bowl with plastic wrap, place it in the refrigerator, and marinate for at least 6 hours. If time allows, let the meat marinate overnight.
5. Remove the meat from the refrigerator and give it a stir.
6. To prepare the jerky in a dehydrator, arrange the meat on the dehydrator trays, making sure to leave space between each piece. Place it in the dehydrator and dehydrate until the meat has dried out but is still flexible, 4 to 6 hours.
7. To prepare the jerky in an oven, preheat the oven to 175°F. Line two rimmed baking sheets with aluminum foil and place wire racks over the foil. Arrange the strips of meat on the racks, making sure to leave space between each piece and to keep the meat in a single layer. Place the pans in the oven and bake for 1½ hours. Rotate the pans and then bake until the meat is dry to the touch, leathery, and slightly chewy, 1½ to 2½ hours.
8. Store the jerky at room temperature in an airtight container, where it will keep for a few weeks. If you are interested in a longer shelf life for your jerky, place it in a bag and vacuum seal it. Stored in a cool, dry place, the vacuum-sealed jerky will keep for 6 months to 2 years.

CAJUN BEEF JERKY

YIELD: 12 SERVINGS
ACTIVE TIME: 30 MINUTES
TOTAL TIME: 4½ TO 6½ HOURS

If your Cajun seasoning blend is not quite hitting the spot, try incorporating some smoked paprika and/or cayenne pepper into the rub.

INGREDIENTS

2 lbs. beef (top round or bottom round)

1 tablespoon brown sugar

1 teaspoon meat tenderizer

2 teaspoons kosher salt

1 teaspoon black pepper

¼ cup Cajun seasoning blend

DIRECTIONS

1. Trim the meat to remove excess fat. Cut the meat into strips that are between ⅛ and ¼ inch thick, slicing with the grain for a chewier jerky or against the grain for a more tender jerky.
2. Place the remaining ingredients in a mixing bowl and whisk until the mixture is thoroughly combined.
3. Add the meat to the rub and stir until the strips are evenly coated.
4. To prepare the jerky in a dehydrator, arrange the meat on the dehydrator trays, making sure to leave space between each piece. Place it in the dehydrator and dehydrate until the meat has dried out but is still flexible, 4 to 6 hours.
5. To prepare the jerky in an oven, preheat the oven to 175°F. Line two rimmed baking sheets with aluminum foil and place wire racks over the foil. Arrange the strips of meat on the racks, making sure to leave space between each piece and to keep the meat in a single layer. Place the pans in the oven and bake for 1½ hours. Rotate the pans and then bake until the meat is dry to the touch, leathery, and slightly chewy, 1½ to 2½ hours.
6. Store the jerky at room temperature in an airtight container, where it will keep for a few weeks. If you are interested in a longer shelf life for your jerky, place it in a bag and vacuum seal it. Stored in a cool, dry place, the vacuum-sealed jerky will keep for 6 months to 2 years.

TERIYAKI BEEF JERKY

YIELD: 12 SERVINGS
ACTIVE TIME: 30 MINUTES
TOTAL TIME: 10½ TO 24 HOURS

My go-to jerky at the moment. I'm confident it'll become yours as well, once you give it a try.

INGREDIENTS

2 lbs. beef (top round, bottom round, or tenderloin)

2 tablespoons brown sugar

2 tablespoons liquid smoke

¼ cup tamari or soy sauce

1 teaspoon meat tenderizer

2 teaspoons kosher salt

1½ teaspoons black pepper

¼ cup teriyaki sauce

DIRECTIONS

1. Trim the meat to remove excess fat. Cut the meat into strips that are between ⅛ and ¼ inch thick, slicing with the grain for a chewier jerky or against the grain for a more tender jerky.
2. Place the remaining ingredients in a mixing bowl and whisk until the sugar has dissolved and the mixture is thoroughly combined.
3. Add the meat to the marinade and stir until the strips are evenly coated.
4. Cover the bowl with plastic wrap, place it in the refrigerator, and marinate for at least 6 hours. If time allows, let the meat marinate overnight.
5. Remove the meat from the refrigerator and give it a stir.
6. To prepare the jerky in a dehydrator, arrange the meat on the dehydrator trays, making sure to leave space between each piece. Place it in the dehydrator and dehydrate until the meat has dried out but is still flexible, 4 to 6 hours.
7. To prepare the jerky in an oven, preheat the oven to 175°F. Line two rimmed baking sheets with aluminum foil and place wire racks over the foil. Arrange the strips of meat on the racks, making sure to leave space between each piece and to keep the meat in a single layer. Place the pans in the oven and bake for 1½ hours. Rotate the pans and then bake until the meat is dry to the touch, leathery, and slightly chewy, 1½ to 2½ hours.
8. Store the jerky at room temperature in an airtight container, where it will keep for a few weeks. If you are interested in a longer shelf life for your jerky, place it in a bag and vacuum seal it. Stored in a cool, dry place, the vacuum-sealed jerky will keep for 6 months to 2 years.

HONEY & GARLIC BEEF JERKY

YIELD: 12 SERVINGS
ACTIVE TIME: 30 MINUTES
TOTAL TIME: 4½ TO 6½ HOURS

Garlic has an incredible flavor, but in large amounts, it can become too sharp. The honey tempers things just enough that you only see garlic's good side here.

INGREDIENTS

2 lbs. beef (top round or bottom round)

2 tablespoons honey

1 teaspoon meat tenderizer

2 teaspoons kosher salt

1½ teaspoons black pepper

3 tablespoons garlic powder

DIRECTIONS

1. Trim the meat to remove excess fat. Cut the meat into strips that are between ⅛ and ¼ inch thick, slicing with the grain for a chewier jerky or against the grain for a more tender jerky.
2. Place the remaining ingredients in a mixing bowl and whisk until the mixture is thoroughly combined.
3. Add the meat to the rub and stir until the strips are evenly coated.
4. To prepare the jerky in a dehydrator, arrange the meat on the dehydrator trays, making sure to leave space between each piece. Place it in the dehydrator and dehydrate until the meat has dried out but is still flexible, 4 to 6 hours.
5. To prepare the jerky in an oven, preheat the oven to 175°F. Line two rimmed baking sheets with aluminum foil and place wire racks over the foil. Arrange the strips of meat on the racks, making sure to leave space between each piece and to keep the meat in a single layer. Place the pans in the oven and bake for 1½ hours. Rotate the pans and then bake until the meat is dry to the touch, leathery, and slightly chewy, 1½ to 2½ hours.
6. Store the jerky at room temperature in an airtight container, where it will keep for a few weeks. If you are interested in a longer shelf life for your jerky, place it in a bag and vacuum seal it. Stored in a cool, dry place, the vacuum-sealed jerky will keep for 6 months to 2 years.

BLACK PEPPER BEEF JERKY

YIELD: 12 SERVINGS
ACTIVE TIME: 30 MINUTES
TOTAL TIME: 4½ TO 6½ HOURS

Pepper's fruity character gets too little recognition. This pepper-forward jerky aims to change that.

INGREDIENTS

2 lbs. beef (top round or bottom round)

1 tablespoon brown sugar

1 teaspoon meat tenderizer

2 teaspoons kosher salt

1 tablespoon freshly ground black pepper

DIRECTIONS

1. Trim the meat to remove excess fat. Cut the meat into strips that are between ⅛ and ¼ inch thick, slicing with the grain for a chewier jerky or against the grain for a more tender jerky.
2. Place the remaining ingredients in a mixing bowl and whisk until the mixture is thoroughly combined.
3. Add the meat to the rub and stir until the strips are evenly coated.
4. To prepare the jerky in a dehydrator, arrange the meat on the dehydrator trays, making sure to leave space between each piece. Place it in the dehydrator and dehydrate until the meat has dried out but is still flexible, 4 to 6 hours.
5. To prepare the jerky in an oven, preheat the oven to 175°F. Line two rimmed baking sheets with aluminum foil and place wire racks over the foil. Arrange the strips of meat on the racks, making sure to leave space between each piece and to keep the meat in a single layer. Place the pans in the oven and bake for 1½ hours. Rotate the pans and then bake until the meat is dry to the touch, leathery, and slightly chewy, 1½ to 2½ hours.
6. Store the jerky at room temperature in an airtight container, where it will keep for a few weeks. If you are interested in a longer shelf life for your jerky, place it in a bag and vacuum seal it. Stored in a cool, dry place, the vacuum-sealed jerky will keep for 6 months to 2 years.

602969

MONTREAL BEEF JERKY

YIELD: 12 SERVINGS
ACTIVE TIME: 30 MINUTES
TOTAL TIME: 4½ TO 6½ HOURS

Introduced to the Canadian city by Romanian Jewish immigrants, Montreal seasoning carries a smoky flavor that pairs perfectly with beef.

INGREDIENTS

2 lbs. beef (eye round, top round, or bottom round)

1 tablespoon brown sugar

1 teaspoon meat tenderizer

2 teaspoons kosher salt

¼ cup Montreal steak seasoning

DIRECTIONS

1. Trim the meat to remove excess fat. Cut the meat into strips that are between ⅛ and ¼ inch thick, slicing with the grain for a chewier jerky or against the grain for a more tender jerky.
2. Place the remaining ingredients in a mixing bowl and whisk until the mixture is thoroughly combined.
3. Add the meat to the rub and stir until the strips are evenly coated.
4. To prepare the jerky in a dehydrator, arrange the meat on the dehydrator trays, making sure to leave space between each piece. Place it in the dehydrator and dehydrate until the meat has dried out but is still flexible, 4 to 6 hours.
5. To prepare the jerky in an oven, preheat the oven to 175°F. Line two rimmed baking sheets with aluminum foil and place wire racks over the foil. Arrange the strips of meat on the racks, making sure to leave space between each piece and to keep the meat in a single layer. Place the pans in the oven and bake for 1½ hours. Rotate the pans and then bake until the meat is dry to the touch, leathery, and slightly chewy, 1½ to 2½ hours.
6. Store the jerky at room temperature in an airtight container, where it will keep for a few weeks. If you are interested in a longer shelf life for your jerky, place it in a bag and vacuum seal it. Stored in a cool, dry place, the vacuum-sealed jerky will keep for 6 months to 2 years.

MAPLE & PEPPER BEEF JERKY

YIELD: 12 SERVINGS
ACTIVE TIME: 30 MINUTES
TOTAL TIME: 4½ TO 6½ HOURS

Get in step with those in the know: Grade B maple syrup is better than the stuff that's received an A.

INGREDIENTS

2 lbs. beef (eye round, top round, or bottom round)

1 tablespoon brown sugar

1 teaspoon meat tenderizer

2 teaspoons kosher salt

2 teaspoons black pepper

¼ cup pure maple syrup

DIRECTIONS

1. Trim the meat to remove excess fat. Cut the meat into strips that are between ⅛ and ¼ inch thick, slicing with the grain for a chewier jerky or against the grain for a more tender jerky.
2. Place the remaining ingredients in a mixing bowl and whisk until the mixture is thoroughly combined.
3. Add the meat to the rub and stir until the strips are evenly coated.
4. To prepare the jerky in a dehydrator, arrange the meat on the dehydrator trays, making sure to leave space between each piece. Place it in the dehydrator and dehydrate until the meat has dried out but is still flexible, 4 to 6 hours.
5. To prepare the jerky in an oven, preheat the oven to 175°F. Line two rimmed baking sheets with aluminum foil and place wire racks over the foil. Arrange the strips of meat on the racks, making sure to leave space between each piece and to keep the meat in a single layer. Place the pans in the oven and bake for 1½ hours. Rotate the pans and then bake until the meat is dry to the touch, leathery, and slightly chewy, 1½ to 2½ hours.
6. Store the jerky at room temperature in an airtight container, where it will keep for a few weeks. If you are interested in a longer shelf life for your jerky, place it in a bag and vacuum seal it. Stored in a cool, dry place, the vacuum-sealed jerky will keep for 6 months to 2 years.

SRIRACHA BEEF JERKY

YIELD: 12 SERVINGS
ACTIVE TIME: 30 MINUTES
TOTAL TIME: 10½ TO 24 HOURS

The incredibly addictive and versatile sriracha lends its unique zing to this spicy jerky.

INGREDIENTS

2 lbs. beef (eye round, top round, or bottom round)

2 tablespoons brown sugar

2 tablespoons liquid smoke

¼ cup sriracha

1 teaspoon meat tenderizer

2 teaspoons kosher salt

1½ teaspoons black pepper

2 teaspoons chili powder

DIRECTIONS

1. Trim the meat to remove excess fat. Cut the meat into strips that are between ⅛ and ¼ inch thick, slicing with the grain for a chewier jerky or against the grain for a more tender jerky.
2. Place the remaining ingredients in a mixing bowl and whisk until the sugar has dissolved and the mixture is thoroughly combined.
3. Add the meat to the marinade and stir until the strips are evenly coated.
4. Cover the bowl with plastic wrap, place it in the refrigerator, and marinate for at least 6 hours. If time allows, let the meat marinate overnight.
5. Remove the meat from the refrigerator and give it a stir.
6. To prepare the jerky in a dehydrator, arrange the meat on the dehydrator trays, making sure to leave space between each piece. Place it in the dehydrator and dehydrate until the meat has dried out but is still flexible, 4 to 6 hours.
7. To prepare the jerky in an oven, preheat the oven to 175°F. Line two rimmed baking sheets with aluminum foil and place wire racks over the foil. Arrange the strips of meat on the racks, making sure to leave space between each piece and to keep the meat in a single layer. Place the pans in the oven and bake for 1½ hours. Rotate the pans and then bake until the meat is dry to the touch, leathery, and slightly chewy, 1½ to 2½ hours.
8. Store the jerky at room temperature in an airtight container, where it will keep for a few weeks. If you are interested in a longer shelf life for your jerky, place it in a bag and vacuum seal it. Stored in a cool, dry place, the vacuum-sealed jerky will keep for 6 months to 2 years.

HONEY & PEPPER BEEF JERKY

YIELD: 12 SERVINGS
ACTIVE TIME: 30 MINUTES
TOTAL TIME: 4½ TO 6½ HOURS

Sweet and spicy are a great combination, particularly when the gap between them is being bridged by the mild flavor of beef.

INGREDIENTS

2 lbs. beef (top round or bottom round)

2 tablespoons honey

1 teaspoon meat tenderizer

2 teaspoons salt

1 tablespoon freshly ground black pepper

2 tablespoons chili powder

DIRECTIONS

1. Trim the meat to remove excess fat. Cut the meat into strips that are between ⅛ and ¼ inch thick, slicing with the grain for a chewier jerky or against the grain for a more tender jerky.
2. Place the remaining ingredients in a mixing bowl and whisk until the mixture is thoroughly combined.
3. Add the meat to the rub and stir until the strips are evenly coated.
4. To prepare the jerky in a dehydrator, arrange the meat on the dehydrator trays, making sure to leave space between each piece. Place it in the dehydrator and dehydrate until the meat has dried out but is still flexible, 4 to 6 hours.
5. To prepare the jerky in an oven, preheat the oven to 175°F. Line two rimmed baking sheets with aluminum foil and place wire racks over the foil. Arrange the strips of meat on the racks, making sure to leave space between each piece and to keep the meat in a single layer. Place the pans in the oven and bake for 1½ hours. Rotate the pans and then bake until the meat is dry to the touch, leathery, and slightly chewy, 1½ to 2½ hours.
6. Store the jerky at room temperature in an airtight container, where it will keep for a few weeks. If you are interested in a longer shelf life for your jerky, place it in a bag and vacuum seal it. Stored in a cool, dry place, the vacuum-sealed jerky will keep for 6 months to 2 years.

BLACK GARLIC BEEF JERKY

YIELD: 12 SERVINGS
ACTIVE TIME: 30 MINUTES
TOTAL TIME: 10½ TO 24 HOURS

Black garlic is an aged garlic that gets cooked at very low temperatures for an extended period of time. The result of this process is an incredibly deep flavor.

INGREDIENTS

2 lbs. beef (eye round, top round, or bottom round)

2 tablespoons brown sugar

2 tablespoons liquid smoke

¼ cup tamari or soy sauce

1 teaspoon meat tenderizer

2 teaspoons kosher salt

1½ teaspoons black pepper

5 black garlic cloves, minced

2 teaspoons paprika

DIRECTIONS

1. Trim the meat to remove excess fat. Cut the meat into strips that are between ⅛ and ¼ inch thick, slicing with the grain for a chewier jerky or against the grain for a more tender jerky.
2. Place the remaining ingredients in a mixing bowl and whisk until the sugar has dissolved and the mixture is thoroughly combined.
3. Add the meat to the marinade and stir until the strips are evenly coated.
4. Cover the bowl with plastic wrap, place it in the refrigerator, and marinate for at least 6 hours. If time allows, let the meat marinate overnight.
5. Remove the meat from the refrigerator and give it a stir.
6. To prepare the jerky in a dehydrator, arrange the meat on the dehydrator trays, making sure to leave space between each piece. Place it in the dehydrator and dehydrate until the meat has dried out but is still flexible, 4 to 6 hours.
7. To prepare the jerky in an oven, preheat the oven to 175°F. Line two rimmed baking sheets with aluminum foil and place wire racks over the foil. Arrange the strips of meat on the racks, making sure to leave space between each piece and to keep the meat in a single layer. Place the pans in the oven and bake for 1½ hours. Rotate the pans and then bake until the meat is dry to the touch, leathery, and slightly chewy, 1½ to 2½ hours.
8. Store the jerky at room temperature in an airtight container, where it will keep for a few weeks. If you are interested in a longer shelf life for your jerky, place it in a bag and vacuum seal it. Stored in a cool, dry place, the vacuum-sealed jerky will keep for 6 months to 2 years.

CURRY BEEF JERKY

YIELD: 12 SERVINGS
ACTIVE TIME: 10 MINUTES
TOTAL TIME: 4½ TO 6½ HOURS

If you want to kick the flavor up even more here, use Madras curry powder, which has a bit more spice than traditional curry powders.

INGREDIENTS

2 lbs. beef (top round or bottom round)

2 tablespoons brown sugar

1 teaspoon meat tenderizer

2 teaspoons kosher salt

1½ teaspoons black pepper

2 tablespoons curry powder

DIRECTIONS

1. Trim the meat to remove excess fat. Cut the meat into strips that are between ⅛ and ¼ inch thick, slicing with the grain for a chewier jerky or against the grain for a more tender jerky.
2. Place the remaining ingredients in a mixing bowl and whisk until the mixture is thoroughly combined.
3. Add the meat to the rub and stir until the strips are evenly coated.
4. To prepare the jerky in a dehydrator, arrange the meat on the dehydrator trays, making sure to leave space between each piece. Place it in the dehydrator and dehydrate until the meat has dried out but is still flexible, 4 to 6 hours.
5. To prepare the jerky in an oven, preheat the oven to 175°F. Line two rimmed baking sheets with aluminum foil and place wire racks over the foil. Arrange the strips of meat on the racks, making sure to leave space between each piece and to keep the meat in a single layer. Place the pans in the oven and bake for 1½ hours. Rotate the pans and then bake until the meat is dry to the touch, leathery, and slightly chewy, 1½ to 2½ hours.
6. Store the jerky at room temperature in an airtight container, where it will keep for a few weeks. If you are interested in a longer shelf life for your jerky, place it in a bag and vacuum seal it. Stored in a cool, dry place, the vacuum-sealed jerky will keep for 6 months to 2 years.

TRIPLE PEPPER BEEF JERKY

YIELD: 12 SERVINGS
ACTIVE TIME: 30 MINUTES
TOTAL TIME: 4½ TO 6½ HOURS

The mysterious buzzing sensation provided by Sichuan peppercorns makes this straightforward jerky one of the most memorable in the book.

INGREDIENTS

2 lbs. beef (top round or bottom round)

1½ teaspoons black peppercorns

1½ teaspoons red peppercorns

1½ teaspoons Sichuan peppercorns

1 tablespoon brown sugar

2 teaspoons kosher salt

DIRECTIONS

1 Trim the meat to remove excess fat. Cut the meat into strips that are between ⅛ and ¼ inch thick, slicing with the grain for a chewier jerky or against the grain for a more tender jerky.

2 Using a mortar and pestle, grind the peppercorns and place them in a mixing bowl. Add the brown sugar and salt and whisk until the mixture is thoroughly combined.

3 Add the meat to the rub and stir until the strips are evenly coated.

4 To prepare the jerky in a dehydrator, arrange the meat on the dehydrator trays, making sure to leave space between each piece. Place it in the dehydrator and dehydrate until the meat has dried out but is still flexible, 4 to 6 hours.

5 To prepare the jerky in an oven, preheat the oven to 175°F. Line two rimmed baking sheets with aluminum foil and place wire racks over the foil. Arrange the strips of meat on the racks, making sure to leave space between each piece and to keep the meat in a single layer. Place the pans in the oven and bake for 1½ hours. Rotate the pans and then bake until the meat is dry to the touch, leathery, and slightly chewy, 1½ to 2½ hours.

6 Store the jerky at room temperature in an airtight container, where it will keep for a few weeks. If you are interested in a longer shelf life for your jerky, place it in a bag and vacuum seal it. Stored in a cool, dry place, the vacuum-sealed jerky will keep for 6 months to 2 years.

JALAPEÑO BEEF JERKY

YIELD: 12 SERVINGS
ACTIVE TIME: 30 MINUTES
TOTAL TIME: 4½ TO 6½ HOURS

Feel free to substitute any dried chiles for the jalapeños here.

INGREDIENTS

2 lbs. beef (top round or bottom round)

6 dried jalapeño chile peppers

1 tablespoon brown sugar

1 teaspoon meat tenderizer

2 teaspoons kosher salt

1½ teaspoons black pepper

DIRECTIONS

1. Trim the meat to remove excess fat. Cut the meat into strips that are between ⅛ and ¼ inch thick, slicing with the grain for a chewier jerky or against the grain for a more tender jerky.
2. Using a mortar and pestle, grind the jalapeños into a fine powder and place them in a mixing bowl. Add the remaining ingredients and whisk until the mixture is thoroughly combined.
3. Add the meat to the rub and stir until the strips are evenly coated.
4. To prepare the jerky in a dehydrator, arrange the meat on the dehydrator trays, making sure to leave space between each piece. Place it in the dehydrator and dehydrate until the meat has dried out but is still flexible, 4 to 6 hours.
5. To prepare the jerky in an oven, preheat the oven to 175°F. Line two rimmed baking sheets with aluminum foil and place wire racks over the foil. Arrange the strips of meat on the racks, making sure to leave space between each piece and to keep the meat in a single layer. Place the pans in the oven and bake for 1½ hours. Rotate the pans and then bake until the meat is dry to the touch, leathery, and slightly chewy, 1½ to 2½ hours.
6. Store the jerky at room temperature in an airtight container, where it will keep for a few weeks. If you are interested in a longer shelf life for your jerky, place it in a bag and vacuum seal it. Stored in a cool, dry place, the vacuum-sealed jerky will keep for 6 months to 2 years.

GREEN CHILE BEEF JERKY

YIELD: 12 SERVINGS
ACTIVE TIME: 30 MINUTES
TOTAL TIME: 10½ TO 24 HOURS

Don't hesitate to double or triple the amount of green chiles here—the sweetness of the brown sugar and tamari gives you some margin for error

INGREDIENTS

2 lbs. beef (top round or bottom round)

2 tablespoons brown sugar

2 tablespoons liquid smoke

¼ cup tamari or soy sauce

1 teaspoon meat tenderizer

2 teaspoons kosher salt

1½ teaspoons black pepper

2 tablespoons finely chopped green chile peppers

2 teaspoons paprika

DIRECTIONS

1 Trim the meat to remove excess fat. Cut the meat into strips that are between ⅛ and ¼ inch thick, slicing with the grain for a chewier jerky or against the grain for a more tender jerky.

2 Place the remaining ingredients in a mixing bowl and whisk until the sugar has dissolved and the mixture is thoroughly combined.

3 Add the meat to the marinade and stir until the strips are evenly coated.

4 Cover the bowl with plastic wrap, place it in the refrigerator, and marinate for at least 6 hours. If time allows, let the meat marinate overnight.

5 Remove the meat from the refrigerator and give it a stir.

6 To prepare the jerky in a dehydrator, arrange the meat on the dehydrator trays, making sure to leave space between each piece. Place it in the dehydrator and dehydrate until the meat has dried out but is still flexible, 4 to 6 hours.

7 To prepare the jerky in an oven, preheat the oven to 175°F. Line two rimmed baking sheets with aluminum foil and place wire racks over the foil. Arrange the strips of meat on the racks, making sure to leave space between each piece and to keep the meat in a single layer. Place the pans in the oven and bake for 1½ hours. Rotate the pans and then bake until the meat is dry to the touch, leathery, and slightly chewy, 1½ to 2½ hours.

8 Store the jerky at room temperature in an airtight container, where it will keep for a few weeks. If you are interested in a longer shelf life for your jerky, place it in a bag and vacuum seal it. Stored in a cool, dry place, the vacuum-sealed jerky will keep for 6 months to 2 years.

HOT
WITH CHILIES

HOT HONEY BEEF JERKY

YIELD: 12 SERVINGS
ACTIVE TIME: 30 MINUTES
TOTAL TIME: 10½ TO 24 HOURS

Mike's Hot Honey is a wonderful product that is well worth tracking down, but if you want to make a spicy honey at home, just simmer four habaneros and 1 cup of honey for 30 minutes, strain, and use as desired.

INGREDIENTS

2 lbs. beef (eye round, top round, or bottom round)

½ cup Mike's Hot Honey

1 teaspoon meat tenderizer

2 teaspoons kosher salt

1½ teaspoons black pepper

2 teaspoons paprika

DIRECTIONS

1. Trim the meat to remove excess fat. Cut the meat into strips that are between ⅛ and ¼ inch thick, slicing with the grain for a chewier jerky or against the grain for a more tender jerky.
2. Place the remaining ingredients in a mixing bowl and whisk until the mixture is thoroughly combined.
3. Add the meat to the marinade and stir until the strips are evenly coated.
4. Cover the bowl with plastic wrap, place it in the refrigerator, and marinate for at least 6 hours. If time allows, let the meat marinate overnight.
5. Remove the meat from the refrigerator and give it a stir.
6. To prepare the jerky in a dehydrator, arrange the meat on the dehydrator trays, making sure to leave space between each piece. Place it in the dehydrator and dehydrate until the meat has dried out but is still flexible, 4 to 6 hours.
7. To prepare the jerky in an oven, preheat the oven to 175°F. Line two rimmed baking sheets with aluminum foil and place wire racks over the foil. Arrange the strips of meat on the racks, making sure to leave space between each piece and to keep the meat in a single layer. Place the pans in the oven and bake for 1½ hours. Rotate the pans and then bake until the meat is dry to the touch, leathery, and slightly chewy, 1½ to 2½ hours.
8. Store the jerky at room temperature in an airtight container, where it will keep for a few weeks. If you are interested in a longer shelf life for your jerky, place it in a bag and vacuum seal it. Stored in a cool, dry place, the vacuum-sealed jerky will keep for 6 months to 2 years.

BLACK PEPPER & CURRY BEEF JERKY

YIELD: 12 SERVINGS
ACTIVE TIME: 30 MINUTES
TOTAL TIME: 10½ TO 24 HOURS

Japanese golden curry leans into the cumin and ginger elements more than traditional curry powders, giving it an earthier and spicier flavor.

INGREDIENTS

2 lbs. beef (top round or bottom round)

2 tablespoons brown sugar

2 tablespoons liquid smoke

¼ cup tamari or soy sauce

1 teaspoon meat tenderizer

2 teaspoons kosher salt

1½ teaspoons black pepper

2 tablespoons Japanese golden curry

2 teaspoons paprika

DIRECTIONS

1. Trim the meat to remove excess fat. Cut the meat into strips that are between ⅛ and ¼ inch thick, slicing with the grain for a chewier jerky or against the grain for a more tender jerky.
2. Place the remaining ingredients in a mixing bowl and whisk until the sugar has dissolved and the mixture is thoroughly combined.
3. Add the meat to the marinade and stir until the strips are evenly coated.
4. Cover the bowl with plastic wrap, place it in the refrigerator, and marinate for at least 6 hours. If time allows, let the meat marinate overnight.
5. Remove the meat from the refrigerator and give it a stir.
6. To prepare the jerky in a dehydrator, arrange the meat on the dehydrator trays, making sure to leave space between each piece. Place it in the dehydrator and dehydrate until the meat has dried out but is still flexible, 4 to 6 hours.
7. To prepare the jerky in an oven, preheat the oven to 175°F. Line two rimmed baking sheets with aluminum foil and place wire racks over the foil. Arrange the strips of meat on the racks, making sure to leave space between each piece and to keep the meat in a single layer. Place the pans in the oven and bake for 1½ hours. Rotate the pans and then bake until the meat is dry to the touch, leathery, and slightly chewy, 1½ to 2½ hours.
8. Store the jerky at room temperature in an airtight container, where it will keep for a few weeks. If you are interested in a longer shelf life for your jerky, place it in a bag and vacuum seal it. Stored in a cool, dry place, the vacuum-sealed jerky will keep for 6 months to 2 years.

HABANERO BEEF JERKY

YIELD: 12 SERVINGS
ACTIVE TIME: 30 MINUTES
TOTAL TIME: 4½ TO 6½ HOURS

Don't make the common mistake of letting the habanero's spice completely overshadow its fruity and subtly smoky flavor.

INGREDIENTS

2 lbs. beef (top round or bottom round)

6 dried habanero chile peppers

1 tablespoon brown sugar

2 teaspoons kosher salt

1 teaspoon paprika

DIRECTIONS

1 Trim the meat to remove excess fat. Cut the meat into strips that are between ⅛ and ¼ inch thick, slicing with the grain for a chewier jerky or against the grain for a more tender jerky.

2 Using a mortar and pestle, grind the habaneros and place them in a mixing bowl. Add the remaining ingredients and whisk until the mixture is thoroughly combined.

3 Add the meat to the rub and stir until the strips are evenly coated.

4 To prepare the jerky in a dehydrator, arrange the meat on the dehydrator trays, making sure to leave space between each piece. Place it in the dehydrator and dehydrate until the meat has dried out but is still flexible, 4 to 6 hours.

5 To prepare the jerky in an oven, preheat the oven to 175°F. Line two rimmed baking sheets with aluminum foil and place wire racks over the foil. Arrange the strips of meat on the racks, making sure to leave space between each piece and to keep the meat in a single layer. Place the pans in the oven and bake for 1½ hours. Rotate the pans and then bake until the meat is dry to the touch, leathery, and slightly chewy, 1½ to 2½ hours.

6 Store the jerky at room temperature in an airtight container, where it will keep for a few weeks. If you are interested in a longer shelf life for your jerky, place it in a bag and vacuum seal it. Stored in a cool, dry place, the vacuum-sealed jerky will keep for 6 months to 2 years.

CLASSIC BBQ BEEF JERKY

YIELD: 12 SERVINGS
ACTIVE TIME: 30 MINUTES
TOTAL TIME: 10½ TO 24 HOURS

A barbecue sauce leaning toward the vinegary side of the spectrum will serve you well here.

INGREDIENTS

2 lbs. beef (top round or bottom round)

½ cup barbecue sauce

2 teaspoons kosher salt

2 teaspoons black pepper

2 teaspoons paprika

DIRECTIONS

1. Trim the meat to remove excess fat. Cut the meat into strips that are between ⅛ and ¼ inch thick, slicing with the grain for a chewier jerky or against the grain for a more tender jerky.
2. Place the remaining ingredients in a mixing bowl and whisk until the mixture is thoroughly combined.
3. Add the meat to the marinade and stir until the strips are evenly coated.
4. Cover the bowl with plastic wrap, place it in the refrigerator, and marinate for at least 6 hours. If time allows, let the meat marinate overnight.
5. Remove the meat from the refrigerator and give it a stir.
6. To prepare the jerky in a dehydrator, arrange the meat on the dehydrator trays, making sure to leave space between each piece. Place it in the dehydrator and dehydrate until the meat has dried out but is still flexible, 4 to 6 hours.
7. To prepare the jerky in an oven, preheat the oven to 175°F. Line two rimmed baking sheets with aluminum foil and place wire racks over the foil. Arrange the strips of meat on the racks, making sure to leave space between each piece and to keep the meat in a single layer. Place the pans in the oven and bake for 1½ hours. Rotate the pans and then bake until the meat is dry to the touch, leathery, and slightly chewy, 1½ to 2½ hours.
8. Store the jerky at room temperature in an airtight container, where it will keep for a few weeks. If you are interested in a longer shelf life for your jerky, place it in a bag and vacuum seal it. Stored in a cool, dry place, the vacuum-sealed jerky will keep for 6 months to 2 years.

HONEY & JALAPEÑO BEEF JERKY

YIELD: 12 SERVINGS
ACTIVE TIME: 30 MINUTES
TOTAL TIME: 10½ TO 24 HOURS

Honey is a more than equal match for the jalapeño's spice, meaning that even those who typically shy away from sweet-and-spicy foods can partake.

INGREDIENTS

2 lbs. beef (top round or bottom round)

½ cup honey

2 tablespoons liquid smoke

2 tablespoons jalapeño powder

2 teaspoons kosher salt

1 teaspoon onion powder

1 teaspoon garlic powder

1½ teaspoons black pepper

2 teaspoons paprika

DIRECTIONS

1. Trim the meat to remove excess fat. Cut the meat into strips that are between ⅛ and ¼ inch thick, slicing with the grain for a chewier jerky or against the grain for a more tender jerky.
2. Place the remaining ingredients in a mixing bowl and whisk until the mixture is thoroughly combined.
3. Add the meat to the marinade and stir until the strips are evenly coated.
4. Cover the bowl with plastic wrap, place it in the refrigerator, and marinate for at least 6 hours. If time allows, let the meat marinate overnight.
5. Remove the meat from the refrigerator and give it a stir.
6. To prepare the jerky in a dehydrator, arrange the meat on the dehydrator trays, making sure to leave space between each piece. Place it in the dehydrator and dehydrate until the meat has dried out but is still flexible, 4 to 6 hours.
7. To prepare the jerky in an oven, preheat the oven to 175°F. Line two rimmed baking sheets with aluminum foil and place wire racks over the foil. Arrange the strips of meat on the racks, making sure to leave space between each piece and to keep the meat in a single layer. Place the pans in the oven and bake for 1½ hours. Rotate the pans and then bake until the meat is dry to the touch, leathery, and slightly chewy, 1½ to 2½ hours.
8. Store the jerky at room temperature in an airtight container, where it will keep for a few weeks. If you are interested in a longer shelf life for your jerky, place it in a bag and vacuum seal it. Stored in a cool, dry place, the vacuum-sealed jerky will keep for 6 months to 2 years.

KOREAN BEEF JERKY

YIELD: 12 SERVINGS
ACTIVE TIME: 30 MINUTES
TOTAL TIME: 10½ TO 24 HOURS

Gochujang is a spicy fermented chili paste that appears in a number of Korean dishes, and will soon be finding its way into more and more of those you prepare at home.

INGREDIENTS

2 lbs. beef (top round or bottom round)

2 tablespoons brown sugar

2 tablespoons liquid smoke

½ cup gochujang

1 teaspoon meat tenderizer

2 teaspoons kosher salt

1 teaspoon garlic powder

1½ teaspoons black pepper

2 teaspoons paprika

DIRECTIONS

1. Trim the meat to remove excess fat. Cut the meat into strips that are between ⅛ and ¼ inch thick, slicing with the grain for a chewier jerky or against the grain for a more tender jerky.
2. Place the remaining ingredients in a mixing bowl and whisk until the sugar has dissolved and the mixture is thoroughly combined.
3. Add the meat to the marinade and stir until the strips are evenly coated.
4. Cover the bowl with plastic wrap, place it in the refrigerator, and marinate for at least 6 hours. If time allows, let the meat marinate overnight.
5. Remove the meat from the refrigerator and give it a stir.
6. To prepare the jerky in a dehydrator, arrange the meat on the dehydrator trays, making sure to leave space between each piece. Place it in the dehydrator and dehydrate until the meat has dried out but is still flexible, 4 to 6 hours.
7. To prepare the jerky in an oven, preheat the oven to 175°F. Line two rimmed baking sheets with aluminum foil and place wire racks over the foil. Arrange the strips of meat on the racks, making sure to leave space between each piece and to keep the meat in a single layer. Place the pans in the oven and bake for 1½ hours. Rotate the pans and then bake until the meat is dry to the touch, leathery, and slightly chewy, 1½ to 2½ hours.
8. Store the jerky at room temperature in an airtight container, where it will keep for a few weeks. If you are interested in a longer shelf life for your jerky, place it in a bag and vacuum seal it. Stored in a cool, dry place, the vacuum-sealed jerky will keep for 6 months to 2 years.

BOURBON BBQ BEEF JERKY

YIELD: 12 SERVINGS
ACTIVE TIME: 30 MINUTES
TOTAL TIME: 10½ TO 24 HOURS

The sweet and slightly charred flavor of bourbon makes it a natural partner with barbecue sauce.

INGREDIENTS

2 lbs. beef (eye round, top round, or bottom round)

2 tablespoons brown sugar

2 tablespoons liquid smoke

¼ cup barbecue sauce

1 teaspoon meat tenderizer

2 teaspoons kosher salt

1½ teaspoons black pepper

2 tablespoons bourbon

2 teaspoons paprika

DIRECTIONS

1. Trim the meat to remove excess fat. Cut the meat into strips that are between ⅛ and ¼ inch thick, slicing with the grain for a chewier jerky or against the grain for a more tender jerky.
2. Place the remaining ingredients in a mixing bowl and whisk until the sugar has dissolved and the mixture is thoroughly combined.
3. Add the meat to the marinade and stir until the strips are evenly coated.
4. Cover the bowl with plastic wrap, place it in the refrigerator, and marinate for at least 6 hours. If time allows, let the meat marinate overnight.
5. Remove the meat from the refrigerator and give it a stir.
6. To prepare the jerky in a dehydrator, arrange the meat on the dehydrator trays, making sure to leave space between each piece. Place it in the dehydrator and dehydrate until the meat has dried out but is still flexible, 4 to 6 hours.
7. To prepare the jerky in an oven, preheat the oven to 175°F. Line two rimmed baking sheets with aluminum foil and place wire racks over the foil. Arrange the strips of meat on the racks, making sure to leave space between each piece and to keep the meat in a single layer. Place the pans in the oven and bake for 1½ hours. Rotate the pans and then bake until the meat is dry to the touch, leathery, and slightly chewy, 1½ to 2½ hours.
8. Store the jerky at room temperature in an airtight container, where it will keep for a few weeks. If you are interested in a longer shelf life for your jerky, place it in a bag and vacuum seal it. Stored in a cool, dry place, the vacuum-sealed jerky will keep for 6 months to 2 years.

BBQ & RYE BEEF JERKY

YIELD: 12 SERVINGS
ACTIVE TIME: 30 MINUTES
TOTAL TIME: 10½ TO 24 HOURS

Rye whiskey is sweet like bourbon, but also spicier.

INGREDIENTS

2 lbs. beef (top round or bottom round)

2 tablespoons brown sugar

¼ cup barbecue sauce

1 teaspoon meat tenderizer

2 teaspoons salt

1½ teaspoons black pepper

2 tablespoons rye whiskey

2 teaspoons paprika

DIRECTIONS

1. Trim the meat to remove excess fat. Cut the meat into strips that are between ⅛ and ¼ inch thick, slicing with the grain for a chewier jerky or against the grain for a more tender jerky.
2. Place the remaining ingredients in a mixing bowl and whisk until the sugar has dissolved and the mixture is thoroughly combined.
3. Add the meat to the marinade and stir until the strips are evenly coated.
4. Cover the bowl with plastic wrap, place it in the refrigerator, and marinate for at least 6 hours. If time allows, let the meat marinate overnight.
5. Remove the meat from the refrigerator and give it a stir.
6. To prepare the jerky in a dehydrator, arrange the meat on the dehydrator trays, making sure to leave space between each piece. Place it in the dehydrator and dehydrate until the meat has dried out but is still flexible, 4 to 6 hours.
7. To prepare the jerky in an oven, preheat the oven to 175°F. Line two rimmed baking sheets with aluminum foil and place wire racks over the foil. Arrange the strips of meat on the racks, making sure to leave space between each piece and to keep the meat in a single layer. Place the pans in the oven and bake for 1½ hours. Rotate the pans and then bake until the meat is dry to the touch, leathery, and slightly chewy, 1½ to 2½ hours.
8. Store the jerky at room temperature in an airtight container, where it will keep for a few weeks. If you are interested in a longer shelf life for your jerky, place it in a bag and vacuum seal it. Stored in a cool, dry place, the vacuum-sealed jerky will keep for 6 months to 2 years.

SWEET & SPICY BEEF JERKY

YIELD: 12 SERVINGS
ACTIVE TIME: 30 MINUTES
TOTAL TIME: 10½ TO 24 HOURS

That warmth you're enjoying isn't just coming from the chili powder—molasses also has a warming quality.

INGREDIENTS

2 lbs. beef (eye round, top round, or bottom round)

¼ cup molasses

2 tablespoons liquid smoke

1 teaspoon meat tenderizer

2 teaspoons kosher salt

1½ teaspoons black pepper

2 teaspoons chili powder

DIRECTIONS

1. Trim the meat to remove excess fat. Cut the meat into strips that are between ⅛ and ¼ inch thick, slicing with the grain for a chewier jerky or against the grain for a more tender jerky.
2. Place the remaining ingredients in a mixing bowl and whisk until the mixture is thoroughly combined.
3. Add the meat to the marinade and stir until the strips are evenly coated.
4. Cover the bowl with plastic wrap, place it in the refrigerator, and marinate for at least 6 hours. If time allows, let the meat marinate overnight.
5. Remove the meat from the refrigerator and give it a stir.
6. To prepare the jerky in a dehydrator, arrange the meat on the dehydrator trays, making sure to leave space between each piece. Place it in the dehydrator and dehydrate until the meat has dried out but is still flexible, 4 to 6 hours.
7. To prepare the jerky in an oven, preheat the oven to 175°F. Line two rimmed baking sheets with aluminum foil and place wire racks over the foil. Arrange the strips of meat on the racks, making sure to leave space between each piece and to keep the meat in a single layer. Place the pans in the oven and bake for 1½ hours. Rotate the pans and then bake until the meat is dry to the touch, leathery, and slightly chewy, 1½ to 2½ hours.
8. Store the jerky at room temperature in an airtight container, where it will keep for a few weeks. If you are interested in a longer shelf life for your jerky, place it in a bag and vacuum seal it. Stored in a cool, dry place, the vacuum-sealed jerky will keep for 6 months to 2 years.

BERBERE BEEF JERKY

YIELD: 12 SERVINGS
ACTIVE TIME: 30 MINUTES
TOTAL TIME: 4½ TO 6½ HOURS

Berbere is an Ethiopian spice blend that is packed with peppery, tangy flavor.

INGREDIENTS

2 lbs. beef (eye round, top round, or bottom round)

1 tablespoon brown sugar

1 teaspoon meat tenderizer

2 teaspoons kosher salt

1½ teaspoons black pepper

¼ cup berbere seasoning

DIRECTIONS

1. Trim the meat to remove excess fat. Cut the meat into strips that are between ⅛ and ¼ inch thick, slicing with the grain for a chewier jerky or against the grain for a more tender jerky.
2. Place the remaining ingredients in a mixing bowl and whisk until the mixture is thoroughly combined.
3. Add the meat to the rub and stir until the strips are evenly coated.
4. To prepare the jerky in a dehydrator, arrange the meat on the dehydrator trays, making sure to leave space between each piece. Place it in the dehydrator and dehydrate until the meat has dried out but is still flexible, 4 to 6 hours.
5. To prepare the jerky in an oven, preheat the oven to 175°F. Line two rimmed baking sheets with aluminum foil and place wire racks over the foil. Arrange the strips of meat on the racks, making sure to leave space between each piece and to keep the meat in a single layer. Place the pans in the oven and bake for 1½ hours. Rotate the pans and then bake until the meat is dry to the touch, leathery, and slightly chewy, 1½ to 2½ hours.
6. Store the jerky at room temperature in an airtight container, where it will keep for a few weeks. If you are interested in a longer shelf life for your jerky, place it in a bag and vacuum seal it. Stored in a cool, dry place, the vacuum-sealed jerky will keep for 6 months to 2 years.

SALT & PEPPER BEEF JERKY

YIELD: 12 SERVINGS
ACTIVE TIME: 30 MINUTES
TOTAL TIME: 4½ TO 6½ HOURS

A classic, straightforward jerky that will come together quickly.

INGREDIENTS

2 lbs. beef (top round or bottom round)

1 teaspoon meat tenderizer

2½ teaspoons Maldon sea salt

2½ teaspoons black pepper

DIRECTIONS

1. Trim the meat to remove excess fat. Cut the meat into strips that are between ⅛ and ¼ inch thick, slicing with the grain for a chewier jerky or against the grain for a more tender jerky.
2. Place the remaining ingredients in a mixing bowl and whisk until the mixture is thoroughly combined.
3. Add the meat to the rub and stir until the strips are evenly coated.
4. To prepare the jerky in a dehydrator, arrange the meat on the dehydrator trays, making sure to leave space between each piece. Place it in the dehydrator and dehydrate until the meat has dried out but is still flexible, 4 to 6 hours.
5. To prepare the jerky in an oven, preheat the oven to 175°F. Line two rimmed baking sheets with aluminum foil and place wire racks over the foil. Arrange the strips of meat on the racks, making sure to leave space between each piece and to keep the meat in a single layer. Place the pans in the oven and bake for 1½ hours. Rotate the pans and then bake until the meat is dry to the touch, leathery, and slightly chewy, 1½ to 2½ hours.
6. Store the jerky at room temperature in an airtight container, where it will keep for a few weeks. If you are interested in a longer shelf life for your jerky, place it in a bag and vacuum seal it. Stored in a cool, dry place, the vacuum-sealed jerky will keep for 6 months to 2 years.

BLACKENED BEEF JERKY

YIELD: 12 SERVINGS
ACTIVE TIME: 30 MINUTES
TOTAL TIME: 4½ TO 6½ HOURS

Blackened seasoning is similar to Cajun seasoning, only milder.

INGREDIENTS

2 lbs. beef (top round or bottom round)

1 tablespoon brown sugar

¼ cup blackened seasoning

2 teaspoons kosher salt

1½ teaspoons black pepper

DIRECTIONS

1. Trim the meat to remove excess fat. Cut the meat into strips that are between ⅛ and ¼ inch thick, slicing with the grain for a chewier jerky or against the grain for a more tender jerky.
2. Place the remaining ingredients in a mixing bowl and whisk until the mixture is thoroughly combined.
3. Add the meat to the rub and stir until the strips are evenly coated.
4. To prepare the jerky in a dehydrator, arrange the meat on the dehydrator trays, making sure to leave space between each piece. Place it in the dehydrator and dehydrate until the meat has dried out but is still flexible, 4 to 6 hours.
5. To prepare the jerky in an oven, preheat the oven to 175°F. Line two rimmed baking sheets with aluminum foil and place wire racks over the foil. Arrange the strips of meat on the racks, making sure to leave space between each piece and to keep the meat in a single layer. Place the pans in the oven and bake for 1½ hours. Rotate the pans and then bake until the meat is dry to the touch, leathery, and slightly chewy, 1½ to 2½ hours.
6. Store the jerky at room temperature in an airtight container, where it will keep for a few weeks. If you are interested in a longer shelf life for your jerky, place it in a bag and vacuum seal it. Stored in a cool, dry place, the vacuum-sealed jerky will keep for 6 months to 2 years.

CHIPOTLE BEEF JERKY

YIELD: 12 SERVINGS
ACTIVE TIME: 30 MINUTES
TOTAL TIME: 10½ TO 24 HOURS

Chipotles are jalapeños that have been dried and smoked, a process that adds an earthy quality to the jalapeño's familiar flavor.

INGREDIENTS

2 lbs. beef (eye round, top round, or bottom round)

4 oz. can of chipotles in adobo

2 tablespoons brown sugar

2 tablespoons barbecue sauce

1 teaspoon garlic powder

1 teaspoon onion powder

2 teaspoons kosher salt

1½ teaspoons black pepper

1½ teaspoons ancho chile powder

1½ teaspoons red pepper flakes

DIRECTIONS

1. Trim the meat to remove excess fat. Cut the meat into strips that are between ⅛ and ¼ inch thick, slicing with the grain for a chewier jerky or against the grain for a more tender jerky.
2. Place the chipotles in adobo in a blender and puree until smooth. Transfer the puree to a mixing bowl, add the remaining ingredients, and whisk until the sugar has dissolved and the mixture is thoroughly combined.
3. Add the meat to the marinade and stir until the strips are evenly coated.
4. Cover the bowl with plastic wrap, place it in the refrigerator, and marinate for at least 6 hours. If time allows, let the meat marinate overnight.
5. Remove the meat from the refrigerator and give it a stir.
6. To prepare the jerky in a dehydrator, arrange the meat on the dehydrator trays, making sure to leave space between each piece. Place it in the dehydrator and dehydrate until the meat has dried out but is still flexible, 4 to 6 hours.
7. To prepare the jerky in an oven, preheat the oven to 175°F. Line two rimmed baking sheets with aluminum foil and place wire racks over the foil. Arrange the strips of meat on the racks, making sure to leave space between each piece and to keep the meat in a single layer. Place the pans in the oven and bake for 1½ hours. Rotate the pans and then bake until the meat is dry to the touch, leathery, and slightly chewy, 1½ to 2½ hours.
8. Store the jerky at room temperature in an airtight container, where it will keep for a few weeks. If you are interested in a longer shelf life for your jerky, place it in a bag and vacuum seal it. Stored in a cool, dry place, the vacuum-sealed jerky will keep for 6 months to 2 years.

CAROLINA REAPER BEEF JERKY

YIELD: 12 SERVINGS
ACTIVE TIME: 30 MINUTES
TOTAL TIME: 4½ TO 6½ HOURS

Proceed with caution: the Carolina Reaper pepper is one of the hottest in the world. Latex gloves and some form of face covering are strongly recommended for those brave souls who are willing to work with these peppers.

INGREDIENTS

2 lbs. beef (top round or bottom round)

1 tablespoon brown sugar

8 dried Carolina Reaper peppers

2 teaspoons kosher salt

1½ teaspoons black pepper

1 teaspoon garlic powder

1 teaspoon onion powder

1 teaspoon paprika

DIRECTIONS

1. Trim the meat to remove excess fat. Cut the meat into strips that are between ⅛ and ¼ inch thick, slicing with the grain for a chewier jerky or against the grain for a more tender jerky.
2. Place the peppers in a food processor and pulse until finely ground. A covering for your mouth and nose is a good idea when working with these peppers. In any event, do not put your face near the processor, and be extremely careful when handling the peppers and resulting rub.
3. Carefully transfer the ground peppers to a mixing bowl. Add the remaining ingredients and whisk until the mixture is thoroughly combined.
4. Add the meat to the rub and stir until evenly coated.
5. To prepare the jerky in a dehydrator, arrange the meat on the dehydrator trays, making sure to leave space between each piece. Place it in the dehydrator and dehydrate until the meat has dried out but is still flexible, 4 to 6 hours.
6. To prepare the jerky in an oven, preheat the oven to 175°F. Line two rimmed baking sheets with aluminum foil and place wire racks over the foil. Arrange the strips of meat on the racks, making sure to leave space between each piece and to keep the meat in a single layer. Place the pans in the oven and bake for 1½ hours. Rotate the pans and then bake until the meat is dry to the touch, leathery, and slightly chewy, 1½ to 2½ hours.
7. Store the jerky at room temperature in an airtight container, where it will keep for a few weeks. If you are interested in a longer shelf life for your jerky, place it in a bag and vacuum seal it. Stored in a cool, dry place, the vacuum-sealed jerky will keep for 6 months to 2 years.

HICKORY BEEF JERKY

YIELD: 12 SERVINGS
ACTIVE TIME: 30 MINUTES
TOTAL TIME: 10½ TO 24 HOURS

Hickory instantly arouses an expectation of smokiness, but don't let that overshadow its subtle sweetness. This slightly sweet beef jerky is one of my go-to recipes for a delicious, easy jerky. Once you try it, you will know why.

INGREDIENTS

2 lbs. beef (eye round, top round, or bottom round)

2 tablespoons brown sugar

2 tablespoons hickory-flavored liquid smoke

¼ cup tamari or soy sauce

1 teaspoon garlic powder

2 teaspoons kosher salt

1½ teaspoons black pepper

2 tablespoons Worcestershire sauce

2 teaspoons paprika

DIRECTIONS

1. Trim the meat to remove excess fat. Cut the meat into strips that are between ⅛ and ¼ inch thick, slicing with the grain for a chewier jerky or against the grain for a more tender jerky.
2. Place the remaining ingredients in a mixing bowl and whisk until the sugar has dissolved and the mixture is thoroughly combined.
3. Add the meat to the marinade and stir until the strips are evenly coated.
4. Cover the bowl with plastic wrap, place it in the refrigerator, and marinate for at least 6 hours. If time allows, let the meat marinate overnight.
5. Remove the meat from the refrigerator and give it a stir.
6. To prepare the jerky in a dehydrator, arrange the meat on the dehydrator trays, making sure to leave space between each piece. Place it in the dehydrator and dehydrate until the meat has dried out but is still flexible, 4 to 6 hours.
7. To prepare the jerky in an oven, preheat the oven to 175°F. Line two rimmed baking sheets with aluminum foil and place wire racks over the foil. Arrange the strips of meat on the racks, making sure to leave space between each piece and to keep the meat in a single layer. Place the pans in the oven and bake for 1½ hours. Rotate the pans and then bake until the meat is dry to the touch, leathery, and slightly chewy, 1½ to 2½ hours.
8. Store the jerky at room temperature in an airtight container, where it will keep for a few weeks. If you are interested in a longer shelf life for your jerky, place it in a bag and vacuum seal it. Stored in a cool, dry place, the vacuum-sealed jerky will keep for 6 months to 2 years.

GHOST PEPPER BEEF JERKY

YIELD: 12 SERVINGS
ACTIVE TIME: 30 MINUTES
TOTAL TIME: 4½ TO 6½ HOURS

Like playing with fire? Go one step further, and eat it. The precautions recommended for handling the Carolina Reaper pepper are also worth considering here.

INGREDIENTS

2 lbs. beef (top round or bottom round)

8 dried ghost peppers

1 tablespoon brown sugar

2 teaspoons kosher salt

1½ teaspoons black pepper

1 teaspoon garlic powder

1 teaspoon onion powder

1 teaspoon paprika

DIRECTIONS

1. Trim the meat to remove excess fat. Cut the meat into strips that are between ⅛ and ¼ inch thick, slicing with the grain for a chewier jerky or against the grain for a more tender jerky.
2. Place the ghost peppers in a blender or food processor and pulse until finely ground. A covering for your mouth and nose is a good idea when handling the ghost peppers. In any event, do not put your face near the blender, and be extremely careful when handling the peppers and resulting rub.
3. Carefully transfer the ground peppers to a mixing bowl. Add the remaining ingredients and whisk until the mixture is thoroughly combined.
4. Add the meat to the rub and stir until the strips are evenly coated.
5. To prepare the jerky in a dehydrator, arrange the meat on the dehydrator trays, making sure to leave space between each piece. Place it in the dehydrator and dehydrate until the meat has dried out but is still flexible, 4 to 6 hours.
6. To prepare the jerky in an oven, preheat the oven to 175°F. Line two rimmed baking sheets with aluminum foil and place wire racks over the foil. Arrange the strips of meat on the racks, making sure to leave space between each piece and to keep the meat in a single layer. Place the pans in the oven and bake for 1½ hours. Rotate the pans and then bake until the meat is dry to the touch, leathery, and slightly chewy, 1½ to 2½ hours.
7. Store the jerky at room temperature in an airtight container, where it will keep for a few weeks. If you are interested in a longer shelf life for your jerky, place it in a bag and vacuum seal it. Stored in a cool, dry place, the vacuum-sealed jerky will keep for 6 months to 2 years.

MESQUITE BEEF JERKY

YIELD: 12 SERVINGS
ACTIVE TIME: 30 MINUTES
TOTAL TIME: 10½ TO 24 HOURS

Mesquite has a powerful flavor that can overwhelm foods when it is used on the grill or in a smoker. Liquid smoke removes all that unpredictability, allowing novices to enjoy a jerky that tastes as though it was made by a seasoned hand.

INGREDIENTS

2 lbs. beef (eye round, top round, or bottom round)

2 tablespoons brown sugar

2 tablespoons mesquite-flavored liquid smoke

¼ cup tamari or soy sauce

1 teaspoon garlic powder

2 teaspoons kosher salt

1½ teaspoons black pepper

2 tablespoons Worcestershire sauce

2 teaspoons paprika

DIRECTIONS

1 Trim the meat to remove excess fat. Cut the meat into strips that are between ⅛ and ¼ inch thick, slicing with the grain for a chewier jerky or against the grain for a more tender jerky.

2 Place the remaining ingredients in a mixing bowl and whisk until the sugar has dissolved and the mixture is thoroughly combined.

3 Add the meat to the marinade and stir until the strips are evenly coated.

4 Cover the bowl with plastic wrap, place it in the refrigerator, and marinate for at least 6 hours. If time allows, let the meat marinate overnight.

5 Remove the meat from the refrigerator and give it a stir.

6 To prepare the jerky in a dehydrator, arrange the meat on the dehydrator trays, making sure to leave space between each piece. Place it in the dehydrator and dehydrate until the meat has dried out but is still flexible, 4 to 6 hours.

7 To prepare the jerky in an oven, preheat the oven to 175°F. Line two rimmed baking sheets with aluminum foil and place wire racks over the foil. Arrange the strips of meat on the racks, making sure to leave space between each piece and to keep the meat in a single layer. Place the pans in the oven and bake for 1½ hours. Rotate the pans and then bake until the meat is dry to the touch, leathery, and slightly chewy, 1½ to 2½ hours.

8 Store the jerky at room temperature in an airtight container, where it will keep for a few weeks. If you are interested in a longer shelf life for your jerky, place it in a bag and vacuum seal it. Stored in a cool, dry place, the vacuum-sealed jerky will keep for 6 months to 2 years.

SESAME & GARLIC BEEF JERKY

YIELD: 12 SERVINGS
ACTIVE TIME: 30 MINUTES
TOTAL TIME: 4½ TO 6½ HOURS

Slightly nutty, with a bold punch from the garlic, this mix makes for an exceptional jerky.

INGREDIENTS

2 lbs. beef (top round or bottom round)

1 tablespoon brown sugar

2 tablespoons white sesame seeds

2 tablespoons black sesame seeds

2 teaspoons kosher salt

1 tablespoon garlic powder

1½ teaspoons black pepper

DIRECTIONS

1 Trim the meat to remove excess fat. Cut the meat into strips that are between ⅛ and ¼ inch thick, slicing with the grain for a chewier jerky or against the grain for a more tender jerky.

2 Place the remaining ingredients in a mixing bowl and whisk until the mixture is thoroughly combined.

3 Add the meat to the rub and stir until the strips are evenly coated.

4 To prepare the jerky in a dehydrator, arrange the meat on the dehydrator trays, making sure to leave space between each piece. Place it in the dehydrator and dehydrate until the meat has dried out but is still flexible, 4 to 6 hours.

5 To prepare the jerky in an oven, preheat the oven to 175°F. Line two rimmed baking sheets with aluminum foil and place wire racks over the foil. Arrange the strips of meat on the racks, making sure to leave space between each piece and to keep the meat in a single layer. Place the pans in the oven and bake for 1½ hours. Rotate the pans and then bake until the meat is dry to the touch, leathery, and slightly chewy, 1½ to 2½ hours.

6 Store the jerky at room temperature in an airtight container, where it will keep for a few weeks. If you are interested in a longer shelf life for your jerky, place it in a bag and vacuum seal it. Stored in a cool, dry place, the vacuum-sealed jerky will keep for 6 months to 2 years.

LEMON PEPPER BEEF JERKY

YIELD: 12 SERVINGS
ACTIVE TIME: 30 MINUTES
TOTAL TIME: 4½ TO 6½ HOURS

The sour-leaning fruitiness of lemon pepper seasoning pairs well with far more than the poultry it so commonly ends up on.

INGREDIENTS

2 lbs. beef (top round or bottom round)

1 tablespoon brown sugar

1 teaspoon garlic powder

2 teaspoons kosher salt

1½ teaspoons black pepper

¼ cup lemon pepper seasoning

DIRECTIONS

1. Trim the meat to remove excess fat. Cut the meat into strips that are between ⅛ and ¼ inch thick, slicing with the grain for a chewier jerky or against the grain for a more tender jerky.
2. Place the remaining ingredients in a mixing bowl and whisk until the mixture is thoroughly combined.
3. Add the meat to the rub and stir until the strips are evenly coated.
4. To prepare the jerky in a dehydrator, arrange the meat on the dehydrator trays, making sure to leave space between each piece. Place it in the dehydrator and dehydrate until the meat has dried out but is still flexible, 4 to 6 hours.
5. To prepare the jerky in an oven, preheat the oven to 175°F. Line two rimmed baking sheets with aluminum foil and place wire racks over the foil. Arrange the strips of meat on the racks, making sure to leave space between each piece and to keep the meat in a single layer. Place the pans in the oven and bake for 1½ hours. Rotate the pans and then bake until the meat is dry to the touch, leathery, and slightly chewy, 1½ to 2½ hours.
6. Store the jerky at room temperature in an airtight container, where it will keep for a few weeks. If you are interested in a longer shelf life for your jerky, place it in a bag and vacuum seal it. Stored in a cool, dry place, the vacuum-sealed jerky will keep for 6 months to 2 years.

KERALA-STYLE BEEF JERKY

YIELD: 12 SERVINGS
ACTIVE TIME: 30 MINUTES
TOTAL TIME: 4½ TO 6½ HOURS

An homage to unakka irachi, a style of dried beef that enjoys a rich tradition in the Indian state of Kerala.

INGREDIENTS

2 lbs. beef (top round or bottom round)

1 tablespoon brown sugar

2 teaspoons turmeric

2 teaspoons kosher salt

1 tablespoon freshly ground black pepper

3 tablespoons chili powder

DIRECTIONS

1. Trim the meat to remove excess fat. Cut the meat into strips that are between ⅛ and ¼ inch thick, slicing with the grain for a chewier jerky or against the grain for a more tender jerky.
2. Place the remaining ingredients in a mixing bowl and whisk until the mixture is thoroughly combined.
3. Add the meat to the rub and stir until the strips are evenly coated.
4. To prepare the jerky in a dehydrator, arrange the meat on the dehydrator trays, making sure to leave space between each piece. Place it in the dehydrator and dehydrate until the meat has dried out but is still flexible, 4 to 6 hours.
5. To prepare the jerky in an oven, preheat the oven to 175°F. Line two rimmed baking sheets with aluminum foil and place wire racks over the foil. Arrange the strips of meat on the racks, making sure to leave space between each piece and to keep the meat in a single layer. Place the pans in the oven and bake for 1½ hours. Rotate the pans and then bake until the meat is dry to the touch, leathery, and slightly chewy, 1½ to 2½ hours.
6. Store the jerky at room temperature in an airtight container, where it will keep for a few weeks. If you are interested in a longer shelf life for your jerky, place it in a bag and vacuum seal it. Stored in a cool, dry place, the vacuum-sealed jerky will keep for 6 months to 2 years.

INDIAN-STYLE BEEF JERKY

YIELD: 12 SERVINGS
ACTIVE TIME: 30 MINUTES
TOTAL TIME: 4½ TO 6½ HOURS

By utilizing a handful of the numerous wonderful spices that are prevalent in the subcontinent, you get a flavor-packed jerky that has quite a kick.

INGREDIENTS

2 lbs. beef (top round or bottom round)

1 tablespoon jaggery or brown sugar

1 teaspoon ground ginger

1 teaspoon garlic powder

2 teaspoons kosher salt

1½ teaspoons black pepper

1 tablespoon chili powder

2 teaspoons garam masala

1 teaspoon turmeric

1 teaspoon cumin

1 teaspoon coriander

DIRECTIONS

1. Trim the meat to remove excess fat. Cut the meat into strips that are between ⅛ and ¼ inch thick, slicing with the grain for a chewier jerky or against the grain for a more tender jerky.
2. Place the remaining ingredients in a mixing bowl and whisk until the mixture is thoroughly combined.
3. Add the meat to the rub and stir until the strips are evenly coated.
4. To prepare the jerky in a dehydrator, arrange the meat on the dehydrator trays, making sure to leave space between each piece. Place it in the dehydrator and dehydrate until the meat has dried out but is still flexible, 4 to 6 hours.
5. To prepare the jerky in an oven, preheat the oven to 175°F. Line two rimmed baking sheets with aluminum foil and place wire racks over the foil. Arrange the strips of meat on the racks, making sure to leave space between each piece and to keep the meat in a single layer. Place the pans in the oven and bake for 1½ hours. Rotate the pans and then bake until the meat is dry to the touch, leathery, and slightly chewy, 1½ to 2½ hours.
6. Store the jerky at room temperature in an airtight container, where it will keep for a few weeks. If you are interested in a longer shelf life for your jerky, place it in a bag and vacuum seal it. Stored in a cool, dry place, the vacuum-sealed jerky will keep for 6 months to 2 years.

CHINESE-INSPIRED BEEF JERKY

YIELD: 12 SERVINGS
ACTIVE TIME: 30 MINUTES
TOTAL TIME: 10½ TO 24 HOURS

Let your inevitable love for this jerky steer you toward the deep history of using dried beef in Chinese culture.

INGREDIENTS

2 lbs. beef (tenderloin, top round, or bottom round)

2 tablespoons brown sugar

2 tablespoons liquid smoke

¼ cup tamari or soy sauce

1 teaspoon Shaoxing wine

2 teaspoons kosher salt

1½ teaspoons black pepper

2 tablespoons hoisin sauce

2 teaspoons paprika

1 teaspoon garlic powder

1 teaspoon ground ginger

2 teaspoons red pepper flakes

DIRECTIONS

1. Trim the meat to remove excess fat. Cut the meat into strips that are between ⅛ and ¼ inch thick, slicing with the grain for a chewier jerky or against the grain for a more tender jerky.
2. Place the remaining ingredients in a mixing bowl and whisk until the sugar has dissolved and the mixture is thoroughly combined.
3. Add the meat to the marinade and stir until the strips are evenly coated.
4. Cover the bowl with plastic wrap, place it in the refrigerator, and marinate for at least 6 hours. If time allows, let the meat marinate overnight.
5. Remove the meat from the refrigerator and give it a stir.
6. To prepare the jerky in a dehydrator, arrange the meat on the dehydrator trays, making sure to leave space between each piece. Place it in the dehydrator and dehydrate until the meat has dried out but is still flexible, 4 to 6 hours.
7. To prepare the jerky in an oven, preheat the oven to 175°F. Line two rimmed baking sheets with aluminum foil and place wire racks over the foil. Arrange the strips of meat on the racks, making sure to leave space between each piece and to keep the meat in a single layer. Place the pans in the oven and bake for 1½ hours. Rotate the pans and then bake until the meat is dry to the touch, leathery, and slightly chewy, 1½ to 2½ hours.
8. Store the jerky at room temperature in an airtight container, where it will keep for a few weeks. If you are interested in a longer shelf life for your jerky, place it in a bag and vacuum seal it. Stored in a cool, dry place, the vacuum-sealed jerky will keep for 6 months to 2 years.

BBQ PORK JERKY

YIELD: 12 SERVINGS
ACTIVE TIME: 30 MINUTES
TOTAL TIME: 10½ TO 24 HOURS

For those who are fans of both jerky and pulled pork.

INGREDIENTS

2 lbs. pork tenderloin

1 tablespoon brown sugar

2 teaspoons kosher salt

1½ teaspoons black pepper

½ cup barbecue sauce

DIRECTIONS

1 Trim the tenderloin to remove any excess fat and silvery skin. Cut the meat into strips that are between ⅛ and ¼ inch thick, slicing with the grain for a chewier jerky or against the grain for a more tender jerky.

2 Place the remaining ingredients in a mixing bowl and whisk until the sugar has dissolved and the mixture is thoroughly combined.

3 Add the meat to the marinade and stir until the strips are evenly coated.

4 Cover the bowl with plastic wrap, place it in the refrigerator, and marinate for at least 6 hours. If time allows, let the meat marinate overnight.

5 Remove the meat from the refrigerator and give it a stir.

6 To prepare the jerky in a dehydrator, arrange the meat on the dehydrator trays, making sure to leave space between each piece. Place it in the dehydrator and dehydrate until the meat has dried out but is still flexible, 4 to 6 hours.

7 To prepare the jerky in an oven, preheat the oven to 175°F. Line two rimmed baking sheets with aluminum foil and place wire racks over the foil. Arrange the strips of meat on the racks, making sure to leave space between each piece and to keep the meat in a single layer. Place the pans in the oven and bake for 1½ hours. Rotate the pans and then bake until the meat is dry to the touch, leathery, and slightly chewy, 1½ to 2½ hours.

8 Store the jerky at room temperature in an airtight container, where it will keep for a few weeks. If you are interested in a longer shelf life for your jerky, place it in a bag and vacuum seal it. Stored in a cool, dry place, the vacuum-sealed jerky will keep for 6 months to 2 years.

HICKORY-SMOKED PORK JERKY

YIELD: 12 SERVINGS
ACTIVE TIME: 30 MINUTES
TOTAL TIME: 10½ TO 24 HOURS

Feel free to substitute your favorite flavor of liquid smoke here.

INGREDIENTS

2 lbs. pork tenderloin

2 tablespoons brown sugar

2 tablespoons hickory-flavored liquid smoke

¼ cup tamari or soy sauce

1 teaspoon garlic powder

2 teaspoons kosher salt

1½ teaspoons black pepper

2 tablespoons Worcestershire sauce

2 teaspoons paprika

DIRECTIONS

1. Trim the tenderloin to remove any excess fat and silvery skin. Cut the meat into strips that are between ⅛ and ¼ inch thick, slicing with the grain for a chewier jerky or against the grain for a more tender jerky.
2. Place the remaining ingredients in a mixing bowl and whisk until the sugar has dissolved and the mixture is thoroughly combined.
3. Add the meat to the marinade and stir until the strips are evenly coated.
4. Cover the bowl with plastic wrap, place it in the refrigerator, and marinate for at least 6 hours. If time allows, let the meat marinate overnight.
5. Remove the meat from the refrigerator and give it a stir.
6. To prepare the jerky in a dehydrator, arrange the meat on the dehydrator trays, making sure to leave space between each piece. Place it in the dehydrator and dehydrate until the meat has dried out but is still flexible, 4 to 6 hours.
7. To prepare the jerky in an oven, preheat the oven to 175°F. Line two rimmed baking sheets with aluminum foil and place wire racks over the foil. Arrange the strips of meat on the racks, making sure to leave space between each piece and to keep the meat in a single layer. Place the pans in the oven and bake for 1½ hours. Rotate the pans and then bake until the meat is dry to the touch, leathery, and slightly chewy, 1½ to 2½ hours.
8. Store the jerky at room temperature in an airtight container, where it will keep for a few weeks. If you are interested in a longer shelf life for your jerky, place it in a bag and vacuum seal it. Stored in a cool, dry place, the vacuum-sealed jerky will keep for 6 months to 2 years.

MAPLE BACON JERKY

YIELD: 12 SERVINGS
ACTIVE TIME: 30 MINUTES
TOTAL TIME: 10½ TO 24 HOURS

As bacon is too fatty to make jerky out of, I came up with this recipe to emulate its unmatched flavor.

INGREDIENTS

2 lbs. pork tenderloin

2 tablespoons liquid smoke

¼ cup tamari or soy sauce

¼ cup pure maple syrup

1 tablespoon kosher salt

1½ teaspoons black pepper

2 tablespoons Worcestershire sauce

2 teaspoons paprika

DIRECTIONS

1. Trim the tenderloin to remove any excess fat and silvery skin. Cut the meat into strips that are between ⅛ and ¼ inch thick, slicing with the grain for a chewier jerky or against the grain for a more tender jerky.
2. Place the remaining ingredients in a mixing bowl and whisk until the mixture is thoroughly combined.
3. Add the meat to the marinade and stir until the strips are evenly coated.
4. Cover the bowl with plastic wrap, place it in the refrigerator, and marinate for at least 6 hours. If time allows, let the meat marinate overnight.
5. Remove the meat from the refrigerator and give it a stir.
6. To prepare the jerky in a dehydrator, arrange the meat on the dehydrator trays, making sure to leave space between each piece. Place it in the dehydrator and dehydrate until the meat has dried out but is still flexible, 4 to 6 hours.
7. To prepare the jerky in an oven, preheat the oven to 175°F. Line two rimmed baking sheets with aluminum foil and place wire racks over the foil. Arrange the strips of meat on the racks, making sure to leave space between each piece and to keep the meat in a single layer. Place the pans in the oven and bake for 1½ hours. Rotate the pans and then bake until the meat is dry to the touch, leathery, and slightly chewy, 1½ to 2½ hours.
8. Store the jerky at room temperature in an airtight container, where it will keep for a few weeks. If you are interested in a longer shelf life for your jerky, place it in a bag and vacuum seal it. Stored in a cool, dry place, the vacuum-sealed jerky will keep for 6 months to 2 years.

HONEY & JALAPEÑO PORK JERKY

YIELD: 12 SERVINGS
ACTIVE TIME: 30 MINUTES
TOTAL TIME: 4½ TO 6½ HOURS

The honey-and-chile-pepper mix really brings out pork's inherent sweetness.

INGREDIENTS

2 lbs. pork tenderloin

2 tablespoons liquid smoke

1 tablespoon jalapeño powder

2 tablespoons brown sugar

1 tablespoon kosher salt

1½ teaspoons black pepper

2 teaspoons paprika

DIRECTIONS

1 Trim the tenderloin to remove any excess fat and silvery skin. Cut the meat into strips that are between ⅛ and ¼ inch thick, slicing with the grain for a chewier jerky or against the grain for a more tender jerky.

2 Place the remaining ingredients in a mixing bowl and whisk until the mixture is thoroughly combined.

3 Add the meat to the rub and stir until the strips are evenly coated.

4 To prepare the jerky in a dehydrator, arrange the meat on the dehydrator trays, making sure to leave space between each piece. Place it in the dehydrator and dehydrate until the meat has dried out but is still flexible, 4 to 6 hours.

5 To prepare the jerky in an oven, preheat the oven to 175°F. Line two rimmed baking sheets with aluminum foil and place wire racks over the foil. Arrange the strips of meat on the racks, making sure to leave space between each piece and to keep the meat in a single layer. Place the pans in the oven and bake for 1½ hours. Rotate the pans and then bake until the meat is dry to the touch, leathery, and slightly chewy, 1½ to 2½ hours.

6 Store the jerky at room temperature in an airtight container, where it will keep for a few weeks. If you are interested in a longer shelf life for your jerky, place it in a bag and vacuum seal it. Stored in a cool, dry place, the vacuum-sealed jerky will keep for 6 months to 2 years.

TURKEY JERKY

YIELD: 10 SERVINGS
ACTIVE TIME: 30 MINUTES
TOTAL TIME: 24 HOURS

It rhymes, it's delicious, it's got it all.

INGREDIENTS

2 lbs. boneless, skinless turkey breasts

2 tablespoons brown sugar

2 tablespoons liquid smoke

¼ cup tamari or soy sauce

2 teaspoons kosher salt

1½ teaspoons black pepper

2 tablespoons Worcestershire sauce

2 teaspoons paprika

DIRECTIONS

1. Slice the turkey breasts into ¼-inch-thick strips.
2. Place the remaining ingredients in a mixing bowl and whisk until the sugar has dissolved and the mixture is thoroughly combined.
3. Add the meat to the marinade and stir until the strips are evenly coated.
4. Cover the bowl with plastic wrap, place it in the refrigerator, and marinate overnight.
5. Remove the meat from the refrigerator and give it a stir.
6. To prepare the jerky in a dehydrator, arrange the meat on the dehydrator trays, making sure to leave space between each piece. Place it in the dehydrator and dehydrate until the meat has dried out but is still flexible, 6 to 8 hours.
7. To prepare the jerky in an oven, preheat the oven to 165°F. Line two rimmed baking sheets with aluminum foil and place wire racks over the foil. Arrange the strips of meat on the racks, making sure to leave space between each piece and to keep the meat in a single layer. Place the pans in the oven and bake for 3 hours. Rotate the pans and then bake until the meat is dry to the touch, leathery, and slightly chewy, 2½ to 3½ hours.
8. Store the jerky at room temperature in an airtight container, where it will keep for a few weeks. If you are interested in a longer shelf life for your jerky, place it in a bag and vacuum seal it. Stored in a cool, dry place, the vacuum-sealed jerky will keep for 6 months to 2 years.

FISH
&
GAME

Those who head to the outdoors in the hopes of procuring food know that once the thrill of a particular conquest has passed, the race is on to make sure all of the meat is utilized.

The recipes in this chapter make that process easier than ever, and also provide hunters and fishermen something substantial to carry along the next time they embark on an excursion.

SALMON JERKY

YIELD: 10 SERVINGS
ACTIVE TIME: 30 MINUTES
TOTAL TIME: 10½ TO 24 HOURS

As you are likely aware, smoke and soy sauce are two of salmon's best friends.

INGREDIENTS

1 lb. salmon fillets

2 tablespoons fresh lemon juice

1 tablespoon brown sugar

2 tablespoons liquid smoke

¼ cup tamari or soy sauce

1 teaspoon garlic powder

2 teaspoons kosher salt

1½ teaspoons black pepper

DIRECTIONS

1. Using tweezers, remove the pin bones from the fillets. Leave the skin on, slice the fillets lengthwise into ¼-inch-thick strips, and cut each strip into 3- to 4-inch pieces.
2. Place the remaining ingredients in a mixing bowl and whisk until the sugar has dissolved and the mixture is thoroughly combined.
3. Add the meat to the marinade and stir until the strips are evenly coated.
4. Cover the bowl with plastic wrap, place it in the refrigerator, and marinate for at least 6 hours. If time allows, let the meat marinate overnight.
5. Remove the meat from the refrigerator and give it a stir.
6. To prepare the jerky in a dehydrator, arrange the meat on the dehydrator trays, making sure to leave space between each piece. Place it in the dehydrator and dehydrate until the meat has dried out but is still flexible, 6 to 8 hours.
7. To prepare the jerky in an oven, preheat the oven to 150°F. Line two rimmed baking sheets with aluminum foil and place wire racks over the foil. Arrange the strips of meat on the racks, making sure to leave space between each piece and to keep the meat in a single layer. Place the pans in the oven and bake for 2½ hours. Rotate the pans and then bake until the meat is dry to the touch, leathery, and slightly chewy, 2½ to 3½ hours.
8. Remove the skin from the pieces of jerky. Store the jerky at room temperature in an airtight container, where it will keep for a few weeks. If you are interested in a longer shelf life for your jerky, place it in a bag and vacuum seal it. Stored in a cool, dry place, the vacuum-sealed jerky will keep for 6 months to 2 years.

HICKORY-SMOKED SALMON JERKY

YIELD: 10 SERVINGS
ACTIVE TIME: 30 MINUTES
TOTAL TIME: 10½ TO 24 HOURS

Using smoke that is a touch sweeter suits salmon jerky quite nicely.

INGREDIENTS

1 lb. salmon fillets

2 tablespoons fresh lemon juice

1 tablespoon brown sugar

2 tablespoons hickory-flavored liquid smoke

1 teaspoon garlic powder

2 teaspoons kosher salt

1½ teaspoons black pepper

DIRECTIONS

1. Using tweezers, remove the pin bones from the fillets. Leave the skin on, slice the fillets lengthwise into ¼-inch-thick strips, and cut each strip into ¾-inch pieces.
2. Place the remaining ingredients in a mixing bowl and whisk until the sugar has dissolved and the mixture is thoroughly combined.
3. Add the meat to the marinade and stir until the strips are evenly coated.
4. Cover the bowl with plastic wrap, place it in the refrigerator, and marinate for at least 6 hours. If time allows, let the meat marinate overnight.
5. Remove the meat from the refrigerator and give it a stir.
6. To prepare the jerky in a dehydrator, arrange the meat on the dehydrator trays, making sure to leave space between each piece. Place it in the dehydrator and dehydrate until the meat has dried out but is still flexible, 6 to 8 hours.
7. To prepare the jerky in an oven, preheat the oven to 150°F. Line two rimmed baking sheets with aluminum foil and place wire racks over the foil. Arrange the strips of meat on the racks, making sure to leave space between each piece and to keep the meat in a single layer. Place the pans in the oven and bake for 2½ hours. Rotate the pans and then bake until the meat is dry to the touch, leathery, and slightly chewy, 2½ to 3½ hours.
8. Remove the skin from the pieces of jerky. Store the jerky at room temperature in an airtight container, where it will keep for a few weeks. If you are interested in a longer shelf life for your jerky, place it in a bag and vacuum seal it. Stored in a cool, dry place, the vacuum-sealed jerky will keep for 6 months to 2 years.

TERIYAKI SALMON JERKY

YIELD: 10 SERVINGS
ACTIVE TIME: 30 MINUTES
TOTAL TIME: 10½ TO 24 HOURS

As any fan of salmon knows, teriyaki's combination of sweet and umami brings out the best in the fish.

INGREDIENTS

1 lb. salmon fillets

2 tablespoons brown sugar

2 tablespoons liquid smoke

¼ cup tamari or soy sauce

2 teaspoons kosher salt

1½ teaspoons black pepper

¼ cup teriyaki sauce

DIRECTIONS

1. Using tweezers, remove the pin bones from the fillets. Leave the skin on, slice the fillets lengthwise into ¼-inch-thick strips, and cut each strip into ¾-inch pieces.
2. Place the remaining ingredients in a mixing bowl and whisk until the sugar has dissolved and the mixture is thoroughly combined.
3. Add the meat to the marinade and stir until the strips are evenly coated.
4. Cover the bowl with plastic wrap, place it in the refrigerator, and marinate for at least 6 hours. If time allows, let the meat marinate overnight.
5. Remove the meat from the refrigerator and give it a stir.
6. To prepare the jerky in a dehydrator, arrange the meat on the dehydrator trays, making sure to leave space between each piece. Place it in the dehydrator and dehydrate until the meat has dried out but is still flexible, 6 to 8 hours.
7. To prepare the jerky in an oven, preheat the oven to 150°F. Line two rimmed baking sheets with aluminum foil and place wire racks over the foil. Arrange the strips of meat on the racks, making sure to leave space between each piece and to keep the meat in a single layer. Place the pans in the oven and bake for 2½ hours. Rotate the pans and then bake until the meat is dry to the touch, leathery, and slightly chewy, 2½ to 3½ hours.
8. Remove the skin from the pieces of jerky. Store the jerky at room temperature in an airtight container, where it will keep for a few weeks. If you are interested in a longer shelf life for your jerky, place it in a bag and vacuum seal it. Stored in a cool, dry place, the vacuum-sealed jerky will keep for 6 months to 2 years.

RAINBOW TROUT JERKY

YIELD: 6 SERVINGS
ACTIVE TIME: 30 MINUTES
TOTAL TIME: 10½ TO 24 HOURS

Rainbow trout's mild, slightly nutty flavor is the perfect vehicle for this sweet and vibrant marinade.

INGREDIENTS

1 lb. rainbow trout fillets

1 tablespoon brown sugar

1 tablespoon liquid smoke

1 teaspoon garlic powder

2 teaspoons kosher salt

1½ teaspoons black pepper

DIRECTIONS

1 Slice the fillets lengthwise into ¼-inch-thick strips and cut each strip into ¾-inch pieces.

2 Place the remaining ingredients in a mixing bowl and whisk until the sugar has dissolved and the mixture is thoroughly combined.

3 Add the meat to the marinade and stir until the strips are evenly coated.

4 Cover the bowl with plastic wrap, place it in the refrigerator, and marinate for at least 6 hours. If time allows, let the meat marinate overnight.

5 Remove the meat from the refrigerator and give it a stir.

6 To prepare the jerky in a dehydrator, arrange the meat on the dehydrator trays, making sure to leave space between each piece. Place it in the dehydrator and dehydrate until the meat has dried out but is still flexible, 4 to 5 hours.

7 To prepare the jerky in an oven, preheat the oven to 150°F. Line two rimmed baking sheets with aluminum foil and place wire racks over the foil. Arrange the strips of meat on the racks, making sure to leave space between each piece and to keep the meat in a single layer. Place the pans in the oven and bake for 2 hours. Rotate the pans and then bake until the meat is dry to the touch, leathery, and slightly chewy, about 2 hours.

8 Remove the skin from the pieces of jerky. Store the jerky at room temperature in an airtight container, where it will keep for a few weeks. If you are interested in a longer shelf life for your jerky, place it in a bag and vacuum seal it. Stored in a cool, dry place, the vacuum-sealed jerky will keep for 6 months to 2 years.

VENISON JERKY

YIELD: 12 SERVINGS
ACTIVE TIME: 30 MINUTES
TOTAL TIME: 10½ TO 24 HOURS

The roast is your best bet when looking to make jerky out of venison.

INGREDIENTS

2 lbs. venison roast

2 tablespoons brown sugar

2 tablespoons liquid smoke

¼ cup tamari or soy sauce

2 teaspoons kosher salt

1½ teaspoons black pepper

2 tablespoons Worcestershire sauce

2 teaspoons paprika

DIRECTIONS

1. Trim the roast to remove any excess fat and silver skin. Cut the meat into strips that are between ⅛ and ¼ inch thick, slicing with the grain for a chewier jerky or against the grain for a more tender jerky.
2. Place the remaining ingredients in a mixing bowl and whisk until the sugar has dissolved and the mixture is thoroughly combined.
3. Add the meat to the marinade and stir until the strips are evenly coated.
4. Cover the bowl with plastic wrap, place it in the refrigerator, and marinate for at least 6 hours. If time allows, let the meat marinate overnight.
5. Remove the meat from the refrigerator and give it a stir.
6. To prepare the jerky in a dehydrator, arrange the meat on the dehydrator trays, making sure to leave space between each piece. Place it in the dehydrator and dehydrate until the meat has dried out but is still flexible, 4 to 6 hours.
7. To prepare the jerky in an oven, preheat the oven to 175°F. Line two rimmed baking sheets with aluminum foil and place wire racks over the foil. Arrange the strips of meat on the racks, making sure to leave space between each piece and to keep the meat in a single layer. Place the pans in the oven and bake for 1½ hours. Rotate the pans and then bake until the meat is dry to the touch, leathery, and slightly chewy, 1½ to 2½ hours.
8. Store the jerky at room temperature in an airtight container, where it will keep for a few weeks. If you are interested in a longer shelf life for your jerky, place it in a bag and vacuum seal it. Stored in a cool, dry place, the vacuum-sealed jerky will keep for 6 months to 2 years.

HICKORY-SMOKED VENISON JERKY

YIELD: 12 SERVINGS
ACTIVE TIME: 30 MINUTES
TOTAL TIME: 10½ TO 24 HOURS

A jerky that will put you beside the campfire in the middle of a three-day camping trip.

INGREDIENTS

2 lbs. venison roast

2 tablespoons brown sugar

2 tablespoons hickory-flavored liquid smoke

¼ cup tamari or soy sauce

1 teaspoon garlic powder

2 teaspoons kosher salt

1½ teaspoons black pepper

2 tablespoons Worcestershire sauce

2 teaspoons paprika

DIRECTIONS

1. Trim the roast to remove any excess fat and silver skin. Cut the meat into strips that are between ⅛ and ¼ inch thick, slicing with the grain for a chewier jerky or against the grain for a more tender jerky.
2. Place the remaining ingredients in a mixing bowl and whisk until the sugar has dissolved and the mixture is thoroughly combined.
3. Add the meat to the marinade and stir until the strips are evenly coated.
4. Cover the bowl with plastic wrap, place it in the refrigerator, and marinate for at least 6 hours. If time allows, let the meat marinate overnight.
5. Remove the meat from the refrigerator and give it a stir.
6. To prepare the jerky in a dehydrator, arrange the meat on the dehydrator trays, making sure to leave space between each piece. Place it in the dehydrator and dehydrate until the meat has dried out but is still flexible, 4 to 6 hours.
7. To prepare the jerky in an oven, preheat the oven to 175°F. Line two rimmed baking sheets with aluminum foil and place wire racks over the foil. Arrange the strips of meat on the racks, making sure to leave space between each piece and to keep the meat in a single layer. Place the pans in the oven and bake for 1½ hours. Rotate the pans and then bake until the meat is dry to the touch, leathery, and slightly chewy, 1½ to 2½ hours.
8. Store the jerky at room temperature in an airtight container, where it will keep for a few weeks. If you are interested in a longer shelf life for your jerky, place it in a bag and vacuum seal it. Stored in a cool, dry place, the vacuum-sealed jerky will keep for 6 months to 2 years.

BBQ VENISON JERKY

YIELD: 12 SERVINGS
ACTIVE TIME: 30 MINUTES
TOTAL TIME: 10½ TO 24 HOURS

Any paprika will do, but smoked paprika is the one you want in this sweet-and-savory jerky.

INGREDIENTS

2 lbs. venison roast

2 tablespoons brown sugar

2 tablespoons hickory-flavored liquid smoke

1 teaspoon garlic powder

2 teaspoons kosher salt

1½ teaspoons black pepper

½ cup barbecue sauce

2 teaspoons paprika

2 teaspoons chili powder

DIRECTIONS

1. Trim the roast to remove any excess fat and silver skin. Cut the meat into strips that are between ⅛ and ¼ inch thick, slicing with the grain for a chewier jerky or against the grain for a more tender jerky.
2. Place the remaining ingredients in a mixing bowl and whisk until the sugar has dissolved and the mixture is thoroughly combined.
3. Add the meat to the marinade and stir until the strips are evenly coated.
4. Cover the bowl with plastic wrap, place it in the refrigerator, and marinate for at least 6 hours. If time allows, let the meat marinate overnight.
5. Remove the meat from the refrigerator and give it a stir.
6. To prepare the jerky in a dehydrator, arrange the meat on the dehydrator trays, making sure to leave space between each piece. Place it in the dehydrator and dehydrate until the meat has dried out but is still flexible, 4 to 6 hours.
7. To prepare the jerky in an oven, preheat the oven to 175°F. Line two rimmed baking sheets with aluminum foil and place wire racks over the foil. Arrange the strips of meat on the racks, making sure to leave space between each piece and to keep the meat in a single layer. Place the pans in the oven and bake for 1½ hours. Rotate the pans and then bake until the meat is dry to the touch, leathery, and slightly chewy, 1½ to 2½ hours.
8. Store the jerky at room temperature in an airtight container, where it will keep for a few weeks. If you are interested in a longer shelf life for your jerky, place it in a bag and vacuum seal it. Stored in a cool, dry place, the vacuum-sealed jerky will keep for 6 months to 2 years.

SWEET & SPICY VENISON JERKY

YIELD: 12 SERVINGS
ACTIVE TIME: 30 MINUTES
TOTAL TIME: 10½ TO 24 HOURS

The unparalleled umami in Worcestershire sauce lends a surprising depth to this jerky.

INGREDIENTS

2 lbs. venison roast

¼ cup honey

2 tablespoons hickory-flavored liquid smoke

1 teaspoon garlic powder

2 teaspoons kosher salt

1½ teaspoons black pepper

2 tablespoons Worcestershire sauce

2 teaspoons paprika

2 tablespoons hot sauce, or to taste

DIRECTIONS

1. Trim the roast to remove any excess fat and silver skin. Cut the meat into strips that are between ⅛ and ¼ inch thick, slicing with the grain for a chewier jerky or against the grain for a more tender jerky.
2. Place the remaining ingredients in a mixing bowl and whisk until the mixture is thoroughly combined.
3. Add the meat to the marinade and stir until the strips are evenly coated.
4. Cover the bowl with plastic wrap, place it in the refrigerator, and marinate for at least 6 hours. If time allows, let the meat marinate overnight.
5. Remove the meat from the refrigerator and give it a stir.
6. To prepare the jerky in a dehydrator, arrange the meat on the dehydrator trays, making sure to leave space between each piece. Place it in the dehydrator and dehydrate until the meat has dried out but is still flexible, 4 to 6 hours.
7. To prepare the jerky in an oven, preheat the oven to 175°F. Line two rimmed baking sheets with aluminum foil and place wire racks over the foil. Arrange the strips of meat on the racks, making sure to leave space between each piece and to keep the meat in a single layer. Place the pans in the oven and bake for 1½ hours. Rotate the pans and then bake until the meat is dry to the touch, leathery, and slightly chewy, 1½ to 2½ hours.
8. Store the jerky at room temperature in an airtight container, where it will keep for a few weeks. If you are interested in a longer shelf life for your jerky, place it in a bag and vacuum seal it. Stored in a cool, dry place, the vacuum-sealed jerky will keep for 6 months to 2 years.

CORIANDER VENISON JERKY

YIELD: 12 SERVINGS
ACTIVE TIME: 30 MINUTES
TOTAL TIME: 10½ TO 24 HOURS

Coriander's fruity and floral character is a wonderful match for rich venison.

INGREDIENTS

2 lbs. venison roast

2 tablespoons brown sugar

2 tablespoons liquid smoke

¼ cup tamari or soy sauce

2 teaspoons kosher salt

1½ teaspoons black pepper

2 tablespoons Worcestershire sauce

1 tablespoon freshly ground coriander seeds

DIRECTIONS

1. Trim the roast to remove any excess fat and silver skin. Cut the meat into strips that are between ⅛ and ¼ inch thick, slicing with the grain for a chewier jerky or against the grain for a more tender jerky.
2. Place the remaining ingredients in a mixing bowl and whisk until the sugar has dissolved and the mixture is thoroughly combined.
3. Add the meat to the marinade and stir until the strips are evenly coated.
4. Cover the bowl with plastic wrap, place it in the refrigerator, and marinate for at least 6 hours. If time allows, let the meat marinate overnight.
5. Remove the meat from the refrigerator and give it a stir.
6. To prepare the jerky in a dehydrator, arrange the meat on the dehydrator trays, making sure to leave space between each piece. Place it in the dehydrator and dehydrate until the meat has dried out but is still flexible, 4 to 6 hours.
7. To prepare the jerky in an oven, preheat the oven to 175°F. Line two rimmed baking sheets with aluminum foil and place wire racks over the foil. Arrange the strips of meat on the racks, making sure to leave space between each piece and to keep the meat in a single layer. Place the pans in the oven and bake for 1½ hours. Rotate the pans and then bake until the meat is dry to the touch, leathery, and slightly chewy, 1½ to 2½ hours.
8. Store the jerky at room temperature in an airtight container, where it will keep for a few weeks. If you are interested in a longer shelf life for your jerky, place it in a bag and vacuum seal it. Stored in a cool, dry place, the vacuum-sealed jerky will keep for 6 months to 2 years.

SPICY VENISON JERKY

YIELD: 12 SERVINGS
ACTIVE TIME: 30 MINUTES
TOTAL TIME: 10½ TO 24 HOURS

Make this as spicy as you can stand, since the flavor will improve as the temperature rises.

INGREDIENTS

2 lbs. venison roast

2 tablespoons brown sugar

2 tablespoons hickory-flavored liquid smoke

¼ cup tamari or soy sauce

1 teaspoon garlic powder

2 teaspoons kosher salt

1½ teaspoons black pepper

2 tablespoons hot sauce, or to taste

2 teaspoons paprika

DIRECTIONS

1. Trim the roast to remove any excess fat and silver skin. Cut the meat into strips that are between ⅛ and ¼ inch thick, slicing with the grain for a chewier jerky or against the grain for a more tender jerky.
2. Place the remaining ingredients in a mixing bowl and whisk until the sugar has dissolved and the mixture is thoroughly combined.
3. Add the meat to the marinade and stir until the strips are evenly coated.
4. Cover the bowl with plastic wrap, place it in the refrigerator, and marinate for at least 6 hours. If time allows, let the meat marinate overnight.
5. Remove the meat from the refrigerator and give it a stir.
6. To prepare the jerky in a dehydrator, arrange the meat on the dehydrator trays, making sure to leave space between each piece. Place it in the dehydrator and dehydrate until the meat has dried out but is still flexible, 4 to 6 hours.
7. To prepare the jerky in an oven, preheat the oven to 175°F. Line two rimmed baking sheets with aluminum foil and place wire racks over the foil. Arrange the strips of meat on the racks, making sure to leave space between each piece and to keep the meat in a single layer. Place the pans in the oven and bake for 1½ hours. Rotate the pans and then bake until the meat is dry to the touch, leathery, and slightly chewy, 1½ to 2½ hours.
8. Store the jerky at room temperature in an airtight container, where it will keep for a few weeks. If you are interested in a longer shelf life for your jerky, place it in a bag and vacuum seal it. Stored in a cool, dry place, the vacuum-sealed jerky will keep for 6 months to 2 years.

TERIYAKI VENISON JERKY

YIELD: 12 SERVINGS
ACTIVE TIME: 30 MINUTES
TOTAL TIME: 10½ TO 24 HOURS

A jerky inspired by my memorable first encounter with venison.

INGREDIENTS

2 lbs. venison roast

2 tablespoons brown sugar

2 tablespoons liquid smoke

¼ cup tamari or soy sauce

2 teaspoons kosher salt

1½ teaspoons black pepper

¼ cup teriyaki sauce

DIRECTIONS

1. Trim the roast to remove any excess fat and silver skin. Cut the meat into strips that are between ⅛ and ¼ inch thick, slicing with the grain for a chewier jerky or against the grain for a more tender jerky.
2. Place the remaining ingredients in a mixing bowl and whisk until the sugar has dissolved and the mixture is thoroughly combined.
3. Add the meat to the marinade and stir until the strips are evenly coated.
4. Cover the bowl with plastic wrap, place it in the refrigerator, and marinate for at least 6 hours. If time allows, let the meat marinate overnight.
5. Remove the meat from the refrigerator and give it a stir.
6. To prepare the jerky in a dehydrator, arrange the meat on the dehydrator trays, making sure to leave space between each piece. Place it in the dehydrator and dehydrate until the meat has dried out but is still flexible, 4 to 6 hours.
7. To prepare the jerky in an oven, preheat the oven to 175°F. Line two rimmed baking sheets with aluminum foil and place wire racks over the foil. Arrange the strips of meat on the racks, making sure to leave space between each piece and to keep the meat in a single layer. Place the pans in the oven and bake for 1½ hours. Rotate the pans and then bake until the meat is dry to the touch, leathery, and slightly chewy, 1½ to 2½ hours.
8. Store the jerky at room temperature in an airtight container, where it will keep for a few weeks. If you are interested in a longer shelf life for your jerky, place it in a bag and vacuum seal it. Stored in a cool, dry place, the vacuum-sealed jerky will keep for 6 months to 2 years.

BLACK PEPPER VENISON JERKY

YIELD: 12 SERVINGS
ACTIVE TIME: 30 MINUTES
TOTAL TIME: 4½ TO 6½ HOURS

The earthy flavors in venison will be amplified by this pepper-forward seasoning blend.

INGREDIENTS

2 lbs. venison roast

2 tablespoons brown sugar

2 tablespoons hickory-flavored liquid smoke

1 teaspoon garlic powder

2 teaspoons kosher salt

1 tablespoon freshly ground black pepper

2 teaspoons paprika

DIRECTIONS

1. Trim the roast to remove any excess fat and silver skin. Cut the meat into strips that are between ⅛ and ¼ inch thick, slicing with the grain for a chewier jerky or against the grain for a more tender jerky.
2. Place the remaining ingredients in a mixing bowl and whisk until the sugar has dissolved and the mixture is thoroughly combined.
3. Add the meat to the rub and stir until the strips are evenly coated.
4. To prepare the jerky in a dehydrator, arrange the meat on the dehydrator trays, making sure to leave space between each piece. Place it in the dehydrator and dehydrate until the meat has dried out but is still flexible, 4 to 6 hours.
5. To prepare the jerky in an oven, preheat the oven to 175°F. Line two rimmed baking sheets with aluminum foil and place wire racks over the foil. Arrange the strips of meat on the racks, making sure to leave space between each piece and to keep the meat in a single layer. Place the pans in the oven and bake for 1½ hours. Rotate the pans and then bake until the meat is dry to the touch, leathery, and slightly chewy, 1½ to 2½ hours.
6. Store the jerky at room temperature in an airtight container, where it will keep for a few weeks. If you are interested in a longer shelf life for your jerky, place it in a bag and vacuum seal it. Stored in a cool, dry place, the vacuum-sealed jerky will keep for 6 months to 2 years.

ALLIGATOR JERKY

YIELD: 6 SERVINGS
ACTIVE TIME: 30 MINUTES
TOTAL TIME: 11½ TO 24 HOURS

As alligator meat is lean, most cuts will work, though I prefer to use meat from the tail when making jerky.

INGREDIENTS

1 lb. alligator meat

1 tablespoon brown sugar

1 tablespoon liquid smoke

1 teaspoon garlic powder

2 teaspoons kosher salt

1½ teaspoons black pepper

DIRECTIONS

1. Trim the meat to remove any excess fat and silver skin. Cut the meat into strips that are between ⅛ and ¼ inch thick, slicing with the grain for a chewier jerky or against the grain for a more tender jerky.
2. Place the remaining ingredients in a mixing bowl and whisk until the sugar has dissolved and the mixture is thoroughly combined.
3. Add the meat to the marinade and stir until the strips are evenly coated.
4. Cover the bowl with plastic wrap, place it in the refrigerator, and marinate for at least 6 hours. If time allows, let the meat marinate overnight.
5. Remove the meat from the refrigerator and give it a stir.
6. To prepare the jerky in a dehydrator, arrange the meat on the dehydrator trays, making sure to leave space between each piece. Place it in the dehydrator and dehydrate until the meat has dried out but is still flexible, 5 to 8 hours.
7. To prepare the jerky in an oven, preheat the oven to 160°F. Line two rimmed baking sheets with aluminum foil and place wire racks over the foil. Arrange the strips of meat on the racks, making sure to leave space between each piece and to keep the meat in a single layer. Place the pans in the oven and bake for 1½ hours. Rotate the pans and then bake until the meat is dry to the touch, leathery, and slightly chewy, 1½ to 2½ hours.
8. Store the jerky at room temperature in an airtight container, where it will keep for a few weeks. If you are interested in a longer shelf life for your jerky, place it in a bag and vacuum seal it. Stored in a cool, dry place, the vacuum-sealed jerky will keep for 6 months to 2 years.

DUCK JERKY

YIELD: 10 SERVINGS
ACTIVE TIME: 30 MINUTES
TOTAL TIME: 24 HOURS

As duck is fatty, you will have to do a little more trimming than normal, but the flavor of the resulting jerky will be well worth the effort.

INGREDIENTS

2 lbs. boneless, skinless duck breasts

2 tablespoons brown sugar

2 tablespoons liquid smoke

¼ cup tamari or soy sauce

2 teaspoons kosher salt

1 teaspoon mushroom powder

1½ teaspoons black pepper

2 tablespoons Worcestershire sauce

2 teaspoons paprika

DIRECTIONS

1. Trim any fat from the duck breasts and slice them into ¼-inch-thick strips.
2. Place the remaining ingredients in a mixing bowl and whisk until the sugar has dissolved and the mixture is thoroughly combined.
3. Add the meat to the marinade and stir until the strips are evenly coated.
4. Cover the bowl with plastic wrap, place it in the refrigerator, and marinate overnight.
5. Remove the meat from the refrigerator and give it a stir.
6. To prepare the jerky in a dehydrator, arrange the meat on the dehydrator trays, making sure to leave space between each piece. Place it in the dehydrator and dehydrate until the meat has dried out but is still flexible, 6 to 8 hours.
7. To prepare the jerky in an oven, preheat the oven to 150°F. Line two rimmed baking sheets with aluminum foil and place wire racks over the foil. Arrange the strips of meat on the racks, making sure to leave space between each piece and to keep the meat in a single layer. Place the pans in the oven and bake for 3 hours. Rotate the pans and then bake until the meat is dry to the touch, leathery, and slightly chewy, 2½ to 3½ hours.
8. Store the jerky at room temperature in an airtight container, where it will keep for a few weeks. If you are interested in a longer shelf life for your jerky, place it in a bag and vacuum seal it. Stored in a cool, dry place, the vacuum-sealed jerky will keep for 6 months to 2 years.

HICKORY-SMOKED ALLIGATOR JERKY

YIELD: 6 SERVINGS
ACTIVE TIME: 30 MINUTES
TOTAL TIME: 11½ TO 24 HOURS

A recipe that hints at just how versatile jerky is.

INGREDIENTS

1 lb. alligator meat

1 tablespoon brown sugar

1 tablespoon hickory-flavored liquid smoke

1 teaspoon garlic powder

2 teaspoons kosher salt

1½ teaspoons black pepper

1 teaspoon paprika

DIRECTIONS

1. Trim the meat to remove any excess fat and silver skin. Cut the meat into strips that are between ⅛ and ¼ inch thick, slicing with the grain for a chewier jerky or against the grain for a more tender jerky.
2. Place the remaining ingredients in a mixing bowl and whisk until the sugar has dissolved and the mixture is thoroughly combined.
3. Add the meat to the marinade and stir until the strips are evenly coated.
4. Cover the bowl with plastic wrap, place it in the refrigerator, and marinate for at least 6 hours. If time allows, let the meat marinate overnight.
5. Remove the meat from the refrigerator and give it a stir.
6. To prepare the jerky in a dehydrator, arrange the meat on the dehydrator trays, making sure to leave space between each piece. Place it in the dehydrator and dehydrate until the meat has dried out but is still flexible, 5 to 8 hours.
7. To prepare the jerky in an oven, preheat the oven to 160°F. Line two rimmed baking sheets with aluminum foil and place wire racks over the foil. Arrange the strips of meat on the racks, making sure to leave space between each piece and to keep the meat in a single layer. Place the pans in the oven and bake for 1½ hours. Rotate the pans and then bake until the meat is dry to the touch, leathery, and slightly chewy, 1½ to 2½ hours.
8. Store the jerky at room temperature in an airtight container, where it will keep for a few weeks. If you are interested in a longer shelf life for your jerky, place it in a bag and vacuum seal it. Stored in a cool, dry place, the vacuum-sealed jerky will keep for 6 months to 2 years.

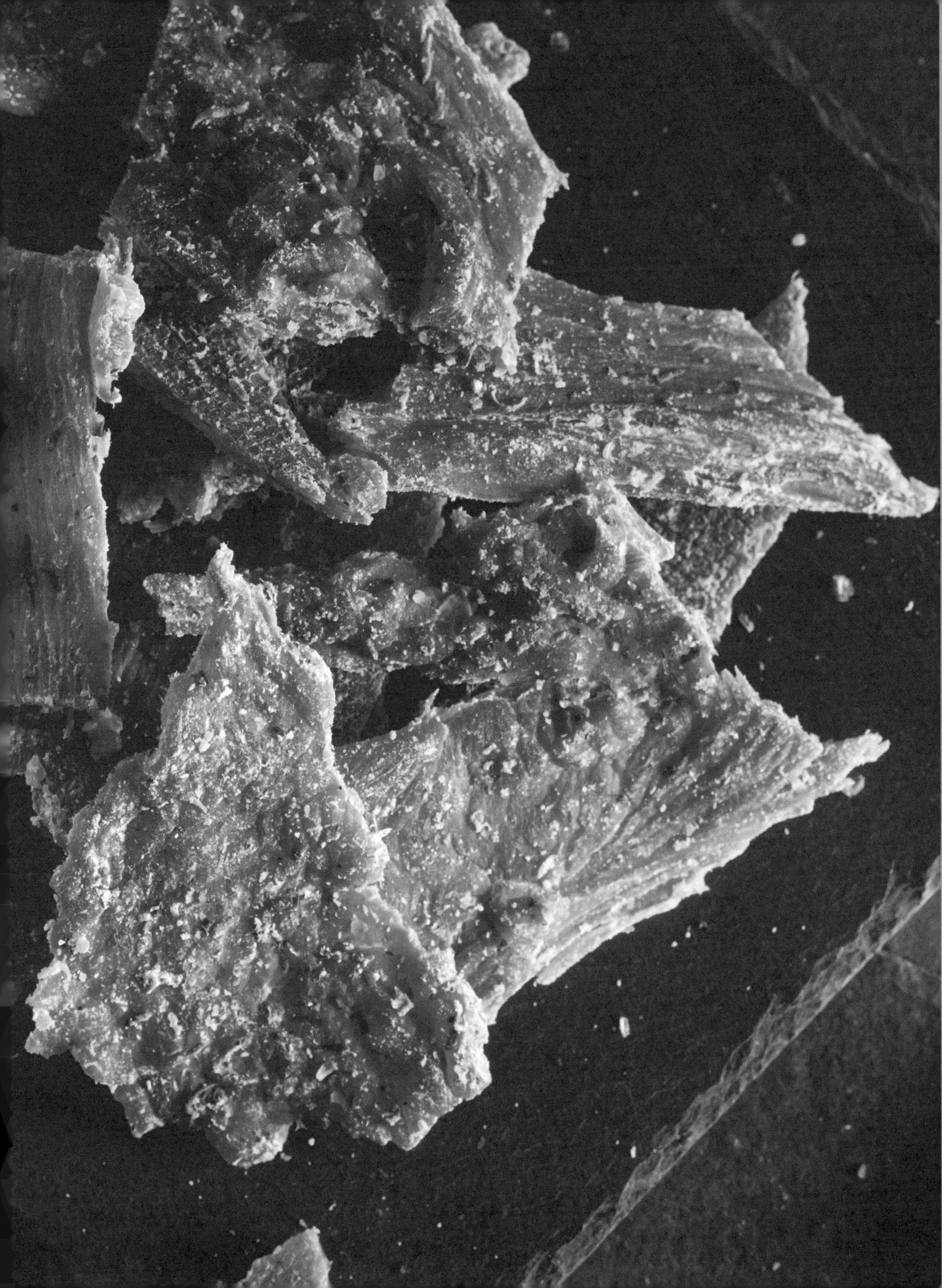

BBQ ALLIGATOR JERKY

YIELD: 6 SERVINGS
ACTIVE TIME: 30 MINUTES
TOTAL TIME: 11½ TO 24 HOURS

If you are so inclined, a tablespoon or two of your favorite hot sauce would suit this preparation quite well.

INGREDIENTS

1 lb. alligator meat

1 tablespoon brown sugar

¼ cup barbecue sauce

1 teaspoon garlic powder

2 teaspoons kosher salt

1½ teaspoons black pepper

DIRECTIONS

1. Trim the meat to remove any excess fat and silver skin. Cut the meat into strips that are between ⅛ and ¼ inch thick, slicing with the grain for a chewier jerky or against the grain for a more tender jerky.
2. Place the remaining ingredients in a mixing bowl and whisk until the sugar has dissolved and the mixture is thoroughly combined.
3. Add the meat to the marinade and stir until the strips are evenly coated.
4. Cover the bowl with plastic wrap, place it in the refrigerator, and marinate for at least 6 hours. If time allows, let the meat marinate overnight.
5. Remove the meat from the refrigerator and give it a stir.
6. To prepare the jerky in a dehydrator, arrange the meat on the dehydrator trays, making sure to leave space between each piece. Place it in the dehydrator and dehydrate until the meat has dried out but is still flexible, 5 to 8 hours.
7. To prepare the jerky in an oven, preheat the oven to 160°F. Line two rimmed baking sheets with aluminum foil and place wire racks over the foil. Arrange the strips of meat on the racks, making sure to leave space between each piece and to keep the meat in a single layer. Place the pans in the oven and bake for 1½ hours. Rotate the pans and then bake until the meat is dry to the touch, leathery, and slightly chewy, 1½ to 2½ hours.
8. Store the jerky at room temperature in an airtight container, where it will keep for a few weeks. If you are interested in a longer shelf life for your jerky, place it in a bag and vacuum seal it. Stored in a cool, dry place, the vacuum-sealed jerky will keep for 6 months to 2 years.

ELK JERKY

YIELD: 12 SERVINGS
ACTIVE TIME: 30 MINUTES
TOTAL TIME: 12½ TO 24 HOURS

As with venison, I prefer to use a roast when making elk jerky, but the tenderloin is another good option.

INGREDIENTS

2 lbs. elk roast

2 tablespoons brown sugar

2 tablespoons liquid smoke

¼ cup tamari or soy sauce

2 teaspoons kosher salt

1½ teaspoons black pepper

2 tablespoons Worcestershire sauce

2 teaspoons paprika

DIRECTIONS

1. Trim the roast to remove any excess fat and silver skin. Cut the meat into strips that are between ⅛ and ¼ inch thick, slicing with the grain for a chewier jerky or against the grain for a more tender jerky.
2. Place the remaining ingredients in a mixing bowl and whisk until the sugar has dissolved and the mixture is thoroughly combined.
3. Add the meat to the marinade and stir until the strips are evenly coated.
4. Cover the bowl with plastic wrap, place it in the refrigerator, and marinate for at least 6 hours. If time allows, let the meat marinate overnight.
5. Remove the meat from the refrigerator and give it a stir.
6. To prepare the jerky in a dehydrator, arrange the meat on the dehydrator trays, making sure to leave space between each piece. Place it in the dehydrator and dehydrate until the meat has dried out but is still flexible, 6 to 8 hours.
7. To prepare the jerky in an oven, preheat the oven to 175°F. Line two rimmed baking sheets with aluminum foil and place wire racks over the foil. Arrange the strips of meat on the racks, making sure to leave space between each piece and to keep the meat in a single layer. Place the pans in the oven and bake for 1½ hours. Rotate the pans and then bake until the meat is dry to the touch, leathery, and slightly chewy, 1½ to 2½ hours.
8. Store the jerky at room temperature in an airtight container, where it will keep for a few weeks. If you are interested in a longer shelf life for your jerky, place it in a bag and vacuum seal it. Stored in a cool, dry place, the vacuum-sealed jerky will keep for 6 months to 2 years.

MAPLE ELK JERKY

YIELD: 12 SERVINGS
ACTIVE TIME: 30 MINUTES
TOTAL TIME: 12½ TO 24 HOURS

Using the more intense flavor of maple sugar enables elk's natural sweetness to reach its apex.

INGREDIENTS

2 lbs. elk roast

2 tablespoons maple sugar

2 tablespoons liquid smoke

2 teaspoons kosher salt

1½ teaspoons black pepper

2 teaspoons chili powder

DIRECTIONS

1 Trim the roast to remove any excess fat and silver skin. Cut the meat into strips that are between ⅛ and ¼ inch thick, slicing with the grain for a chewier jerky or against the grain for a more tender jerky.

2 Place the remaining ingredients in a mixing bowl and whisk until the sugar has dissolved and the mixture is thoroughly combined.

3 Add the meat to the marinade and stir until the strips are evenly coated.

4 Cover the bowl with plastic wrap, place it in the refrigerator, and marinate for at least 6 hours. If time allows, let the meat marinate overnight.

5 Remove the meat from the refrigerator and give it a stir.

6 To prepare the jerky in a dehydrator, arrange the meat on the dehydrator trays, making sure to leave space between each piece. Place it in the dehydrator and dehydrate until the meat has dried out but is still flexible, 6 to 8 hours.

7 To prepare the jerky in an oven, preheat the oven to 175°F. Line two rimmed baking sheets with aluminum foil and place wire racks over the foil. Arrange the strips of meat on the racks, making sure to leave space between each piece and to keep the meat in a single layer. Place the pans in the oven and bake for 1½ hours. Rotate the pans and then bake until the meat is dry to the touch, leathery, and slightly chewy, 1½ to 2½ hours.

8 Store the jerky at room temperature in an airtight container, where it will keep for a few weeks. If you are interested in a longer shelf life for your jerky, place it in a bag and vacuum seal it. Stored in a cool, dry place, the vacuum-sealed jerky will keep for 6 months to 2 years.

SMOKING HOT ELK JERKY

YIELD: 12 SERVINGS
ACTIVE TIME: 30 MINUTES
TOTAL TIME: 12½ TO 24 HOURS

For those hunters who like to keep things spicy when out in the woods.

INGREDIENTS

2 lbs. elk roast

2 tablespoons brown sugar

2 tablespoons hickory-flavored liquid smoke

2 teaspoons kosher salt

1½ teaspoons black pepper

2 teaspoons hot sauce

DIRECTIONS

1 Trim the roast to remove any excess fat and silver skin. Cut the meat into strips that are between ⅛ and ¼ inch thick, slicing with the grain for a chewier jerky or against the grain for a more tender jerky.

2 Place the remaining ingredients in a mixing bowl and whisk until the sugar has dissolved and the mixture is thoroughly combined.

3 Add the meat to the marinade and stir until the strips are evenly coated.

4 Cover the bowl with plastic wrap, place it in the refrigerator, and marinate for at least 6 hours. If time allows, let the meat marinate overnight.

5 Remove the meat from the refrigerator and give it a stir.

6 To prepare the jerky in a dehydrator, arrange the meat on the dehydrator trays, making sure to leave space between each piece. Place it in the dehydrator and dehydrate until the meat has dried out but is still flexible, 6 to 8 hours.

7 To prepare the jerky in an oven, preheat the oven to 175°F. Line two rimmed baking sheets with aluminum foil and place wire racks over the foil. Arrange the strips of meat on the racks, making sure to leave space between each piece and to keep the meat in a single layer. Place the pans in the oven and bake for 1½ hours. Rotate the pans and then bake until the meat is dry to the touch, leathery, and slightly chewy, 1½ to 2½ hours.

8 Store the jerky at room temperature in an airtight container, where it will keep for a few weeks. If you are interested in a longer shelf life for your jerky, place it in a bag and vacuum seal it. Stored in a cool, dry place, the vacuum-sealed jerky will keep for 6 months to 2 years.

HICKORY BUFFALO JERKY

YIELD: 12 SERVINGS
ACTIVE TIME: 30 MINUTES
TOTAL TIME: 12½ TO 24 HOURS

If you like a lot of smoky flavor, consider going with a smoked paprika in this blend.

INGREDIENTS

2 lbs. buffalo flank steak

2 tablespoons brown sugar

2 tablespoons hickory-flavored liquid smoke

1 teaspoon meat tenderizer

2 teaspoons kosher salt

1½ teaspoons black pepper

2 teaspoons paprika

DIRECTIONS

1 Trim the meat to remove any excess fat. Cut the meat into strips that are between ⅛ and ¼ inch thick, slicing with the grain for a chewier jerky or against the grain for a more tender jerky.

2 Place the remaining ingredients in a mixing bowl and whisk until the sugar has dissolved and the mixture is thoroughly combined.

3 Add the meat to the marinade and stir until the strips are evenly coated.

4 Cover the bowl with plastic wrap, place it in the refrigerator, and marinate for at least 6 hours. If time allows, let the meat marinate overnight.

5 Remove the meat from the refrigerator and give it a stir.

6 To prepare the jerky in a dehydrator, arrange the meat on the dehydrator trays, making sure to leave space between each piece. Place it in the dehydrator and dehydrate until the meat has dried out but is still flexible, 6 to 8 hours.

7 To prepare the jerky in an oven, preheat the oven to 160°F. Line two rimmed baking sheets with aluminum foil and place wire racks over the foil. Arrange the strips of meat on the racks, making sure to leave space between each piece and to keep the meat in a single layer. Place the pans in the oven and bake for 4 hours. Rotate the pans and then bake until the meat is dry to the touch, leathery, and slightly chewy, 3 to 4½ hours.

8 Store the jerky at room temperature in an airtight container, where it will keep for a few weeks. If you are interested in a longer shelf life for your jerky, place it in a bag and vacuum seal it. Stored in a cool, dry place, the vacuum-sealed jerky will keep for 6 months to 2 years.

BUFFALO JERKY

YIELD: 12 SERVINGS
ACTIVE TIME: 30 MINUTES
TOTAL TIME: 12½ TO 24 HOURS

When making jerky out of buffalo, I've found that the flank steak strikes the right balance between lean and flavorful.

INGREDIENTS

2 lbs. buffalo flank steak

2 tablespoons brown sugar

2 tablespoons liquid smoke

¼ cup tamari or soy sauce

1 teaspoon meat tenderizer

2 teaspoons kosher salt

1½ teaspoons black pepper

2 tablespoons Worcestershire sauce

2 teaspoons paprika

DIRECTIONS

1. Trim the meat to remove any excess fat. Cut the meat into strips that are between ⅛ and ¼ inch thick, slicing with the grain for a chewier jerky or against the grain for a more tender jerky.
2. Place the remaining ingredients in a mixing bowl and whisk until the sugar has dissolved and the mixture is thoroughly combined.
3. Add the meat to the marinade and stir until the strips are evenly coated.
4. Cover the bowl with plastic wrap, place it in the refrigerator, and marinate for at least 6 hours. If time allows, let the meat marinate overnight.
5. Remove the meat from the refrigerator and give it a stir.
6. To prepare the jerky in a dehydrator, arrange the meat on the dehydrator trays, making sure to leave space between each piece. Place it in the dehydrator and dehydrate until the meat has dried out but is still flexible, 6 to 8 hours.
7. To prepare the jerky in an oven, preheat the oven to 160°F. Line two rimmed baking sheets with aluminum foil and place wire racks over the foil. Arrange the strips of meat on the racks, making sure to leave space between each piece and to keep the meat in a single layer. Place the pans in the oven and bake for 4 hours. Rotate the pans and then bake until the meat is dry to the touch, leathery, and slightly chewy, 3 to 4½ hours.
8. Store the jerky at room temperature in an airtight container, where it will keep for a few weeks. If you are interested in a longer shelf life for your jerky, place it in a bag and vacuum seal it. Stored in a cool, dry place, the vacuum-sealed jerky will keep for 6 months to 2 years.

FRUIT LEATHER & VEGETARIAN JERKY

Jerky is not limited to proteins—fruits and vegetables can also be dehydrated and turned into delicious strips to snack on. In fact, since fruits and vegetables contain so much water, dehydrating them actually amplifies their flavors considerably, concentrating the goodness instilled by Mother Nature.

If you're someone whose green thumb brings forth a considerable bounty each growing season, someone who can't stop themselves from loading up on everything that looks wonderful at the farmers market, or just someone looking for healthier snack options, this chapter has you covered.

BLUEBERRY FRUIT LEATHER

YIELD: 10 SERVINGS
ACTIVE TIME: 1 HOUR
TOTAL TIME: 7 TO 10 HOURS

If you struggle to get your kids to eat fruit, this preparation is here to help.

INGREDIENTS

8 cups blueberries

1 cup water

1 tablespoon sugar, plus more to taste

1 tablespoon fresh lemon juice

DIRECTIONS

1. If using an oven to dehydrate, preheat it to 140°F. Place all the ingredients in a large pot and bring the mixture to a simmer.
2. Cover the pot and simmer until the blueberries are mushy, about 15 minutes.
3. Transfer the mixture to a blender and puree until smooth. Taste the puree and add sugar if desired. If you do add sugar, puree until it is incorporated.
4. Return the mixture to the pot and bring it to a simmer. Cook until the mixture has thickened enough to coat the back of a wooden spoon, about 10 minutes.
5. Line a rimmed baking sheet with a Silpat mat, if using an oven. If using a dehydrator, use a fruit insert. Pour the puree onto the baking sheet or insert until it is an even layer that is approximately ⅛ inch thick.
6. Bake in the oven for 8 to 9 hours; if using a dehydrator, dehydrate for 6 to 8 hours. When the fruit leather is dry, slightly sticky, and chewy, it is ready.
7. Peel the fruit leather off of the mat and cut it into pieces that are the desired shape and size. Store the fruit leather at room temperature in an airtight container, where it will keep for a few weeks. If you are interested in a longer shelf life for your jerky, place it in a bag and vacuum seal it. Stored in a cool, dry place, the vacuum-sealed jerky will keep for 6 months to 2 years.

STRAWBERRY FRUIT LEATHER

YIELD: 10 SERVINGS
ACTIVE TIME: 1 HOUR
TOTAL TIME: 7 TO 10 HOURS

The key to making fruit leather is to be sure to give the juicy mixture plenty of time to dry out.

INGREDIENTS

8 cups strawberries, hulled and sliced

1 cup water

1 tablespoon sugar, plus more to taste

1 tablespoon fresh lemon juice

DIRECTIONS

1. If using an oven to dehydrate, preheat it to 140°F. Place all the ingredients in a large pot and bring the mixture to a simmer.
2. Cover the pot and simmer until the strawberries are mushy, about 15 minutes.
3. Transfer the mixture to a blender and puree until smooth. Taste the puree and add sugar if desired. If you do add sugar, puree until it is incorporated.
4. Return the mixture to the pot and bring it to a simmer. Cook until the mixture has thickened enough to coat the back of a wooden spoon, about 10 minutes.
5. Line a rimmed baking sheet with a Silpat mat, if using an oven. If using a dehydrator, use a fruit insert. Pour the puree onto the baking sheet or insert until it is an even layer that is approximately ⅛ inch thick.
6. Bake in the oven for 8 to 9 hours; if using a dehydrator, dehydrate for 6 to 8 hours. When the fruit leather is dry, slightly sticky, and chewy, it is ready.
7. Peel the fruit leather off of the mat and cut it into pieces that are the desired shape and size. Store the fruit leather at room temperature in an airtight container, where it will keep for a few weeks. If you are interested in a longer shelf life for your jerky, place it in a bag and vacuum seal it. Stored in a cool, dry place, the vacuum-sealed jerky will keep for 6 months to 2 years.

RASPBERRY FRUIT LEATHER

YIELD: 10 SERVINGS
ACTIVE TIME: 1 HOUR
TOTAL TIME: 7 TO 10 HOURS

A way to make berry season last all year long.

INGREDIENTS

8 cups raspberries

1 cup water

1 tablespoon sugar, plus more to taste

1 tablespoon fresh lemon juice

DIRECTIONS

1. If using an oven to dehydrate, preheat it to 140°F. Place all the ingredients in a large pot and bring the mixture to a simmer.
2. Cover the pot and simmer until the raspberries are mushy, about 15 minutes.
3. Transfer the mixture to a blender and puree until smooth. Taste the puree and add sugar if desired. If you do add sugar, puree until it is incorporated.
4. Return the mixture to the pot and bring it to a simmer. Cook until the mixture has thickened enough to coat the back of a wooden spoon, about 10 minutes.
5. Line a rimmed baking sheet with a Silpat mat, if using an oven. If using a dehydrator, use a fruit insert. Pour the puree onto the baking sheet or insert until it is an even layer that is approximately ⅛ inch thick.
6. Bake in the oven for 8 to 9 hours; if using a dehydrator, dehydrate for 6 to 8 hours. When the fruit leather is dry, slightly sticky, and chewy, it is ready.
7. Peel the fruit leather off of the mat and cut it into pieces that are the desired shape and size. Store the fruit leather at room temperature in an airtight container, where it will keep for a few weeks. If you are interested in a longer shelf life for your jerky, place it in a bag and vacuum seal it. Stored in a cool, dry place, the vacuum-sealed jerky will keep for 6 months to 2 years.

MIXED BERRY FRUIT LEATHER

YIELD: 10 SERVINGS
ACTIVE TIME: 1 HOUR
TOTAL TIME: 7 TO 10 HOURS

This mixture of berries gives this fruit leather a perfect combination of sweet and tart.

INGREDIENTS

2 cups strawberries, hulled and sliced

2 cups blueberries

2 cups blackberries

1 cup water

1 tablespoon sugar, plus more to taste

1 tablespoon fresh lemon juice

DIRECTIONS

1. If using an oven to dehydrate, preheat it to 140°F. Place all the ingredients in a large pot and bring the mixture to a simmer.
2. Cover the pot and simmer until the berries are mushy, about 15 minutes.
3. Transfer the mixture to a blender and puree until smooth. Taste the puree and add sugar if desired. If you do add sugar, puree until it is incorporated.
4. Return the mixture to the pot and bring it to a simmer. Cook until the mixture has thickened enough to coat the back of a wooden spoon, about 10 minutes.
5. Line a rimmed baking sheet with a Silpat mat, if using an oven. If using a dehydrator, use a fruit insert. Pour the puree onto the baking sheet or insert until it is an even layer that is approximately ⅛ inch thick.
6. Bake in the oven for 8 to 9 hours; if using a dehydrator, dehydrate for 6 to 8 hours. When the fruit leather is dry, slightly sticky, and chewy, it is ready.
7. Peel the fruit leather off of the mat and cut it into pieces that are the desired shape and size. Store the fruit leather at room temperature in an airtight container, where it will keep for a few weeks. If you are interested in a longer shelf life for your jerky, place it in a bag and vacuum seal it. Stored in a cool, dry place, the vacuum-sealed jerky will keep for 6 months to 2 years.

CARROT JERKY

YIELD: 10 SERVINGS
ACTIVE TIME: 30 MINUTES
TOTAL TIME: 10½ TO 24 HOURS

Everyone will find this jerky delicious. Even better, since it's vegan, everyone is welcome to.

INGREDIENTS

4 large carrots

1 tablespoon extra-virgin olive oil

2 tablespoons coconut aminos

1 tablespoon vegan Worcestershire sauce

1 teaspoon black pepper

2 teaspoons kosher salt

2 tablespoons brown sugar

1 tablespoon chili powder

DIRECTIONS

1. Place all the ingredients, except for the carrots, in a mixing bowl and stir to combine.
2. Peel the carrots and cut them into ¼-inch-thick strips. Add them to the marinade, toss until they are evenly coated, and place them in the refrigerator. Marinate for at least 6 hours. If time allows, marinate the carrots overnight.
3. Remove the carrots from the refrigerator and stir the mixture.
4. To prepare the jerky in a dehydrator, arrange the carrots on the dehydrator trays, making sure to leave space between each piece. Place it in the dehydrator and dehydrate until the carrots have dried out but are still flexible, 6 to 8 hours.
5. To prepare the jerky in an oven, preheat the oven to 140°F. Line two rimmed baking sheets with aluminum foil and place wire racks over the foil. Arrange the carrot strips on the racks, making sure to leave space between each piece and keep the carrots in a single layer. Place the pans in the oven and bake for 1½ hours. Rotate the pans and then bake until the carrots are dry to the touch, leathery, and slightly chewy, 2½ to 4½ hours.
6. Store the jerky at room temperature in an airtight container, where it will keep for a few weeks. If you are interested in a longer shelf life for your jerky, place it in a bag and vacuum seal it. Stored in a cool, dry place, the vacuum-sealed jerky will keep for 6 months to 2 years.

PUMPKIN JERKY

YIELD: 10 SERVINGS
ACTIVE TIME: 30 MINUTES
TOTAL TIME: 6½ TO 12½ HOURS

As you can see, jerky isn't limited to proteins. If you don't have any pumpkin on hand, butternut or Blue Hubbard squash can be substituted.

INGREDIENTS

1 tablespoon extra-virgin olive oil

2 tablespoons coconut aminos

1 tablespoon vegan Worcestershire sauce

1 teaspoon black pepper

2 teaspoons kosher salt

2 tablespoons brown sugar

1 tablespoon chili powder

1 pumpkin (3 to 4 lbs.)

DIRECTIONS

1. Place all the ingredients, except for the pumpkin, in a mixing bowl and stir to combine.
2. Cut the pumpkin in half and scoop out the seeds. Peel the pumpkin and then cut the flesh into ¼-inch-thick strips. Add them to the marinade, toss until they are evenly coated, and place them in the refrigerator. Marinate for 2 to 4 hours.
3. Remove the pumpkin from the refrigerator and stir the mixture.
4. To prepare the jerky in a dehydrator, arrange the pumpkin on the dehydrator trays, making sure to leave space between each piece. Place it in the dehydrator and dehydrate until the pumpkin has dried out but is still flexible, 6 to 8 hours.
5. To prepare the jerky in an oven, preheat the oven to 140°F. Line two rimmed baking sheets with aluminum foil and place wire racks over the foil. Arrange the strips of pumpkin on the racks, making sure to leave space between each piece and to keep the pumpkin in a single layer. Place the pans in the oven and bake for 1½ hours. Rotate the pans and then bake until the pumpkin is dry to the touch, leathery, and slightly chewy, 2½ to 4½ hours.
6. Store the jerky at room temperature in an airtight container, where it will keep for a few weeks. If you are interested in a longer shelf life for your jerky, place it in a bag and vacuum seal it. Stored in a cool, dry place, the vacuum-sealed jerky will keep for 6 months to 2 years.

METRIC CONVERSIONS

U.S. Measurement	Approximate Metric Liquid Measurement	Approximate Metric Dry Measurement
1 teaspoon	5 ml	5 g
1 tablespoon or ½ ounce	15 ml	14 g
1 ounce or ¼ cup	30 ml	29 g
¼ cup or 2 ounces	60 ml	57 g
⅓ cup	80 ml	76 g
½ cup or 4 ounces	120 ml	113 g
⅔ cup	160 ml	151 g
¾ cup or 6 ounces	180 ml	170 g
1 cup or 8 ounces or ½ pint	240 ml	227 g
1½ cups or 12 ounces	350 ml	340 g
2 cups or 1 pint or 16 ounces	475 ml	454 g
3 cups or 1½ pints	700 ml	680 g
4 cups or 2 pints or 1 quart	950 ml	908 g

INDEX

C

ABOUT THE AUTHOR

Keith Sarasin is an author, chef, speaker, and restaurateur. In 2012, Keith started The Farmers Dinner. The Farmers Dinner hosts upscale dinners on local New England Farms. Since 2012, The Farmers Dinner has hosted over 100 farm-to-table events across New England, fed more than 19,000 customers, and raised over $188,000 for local farms.

In addition, Keith has studied Indian food and history for the last 10 years, which led him to starting Aatma. Aatma is an exciting and unique tasting experience that presents food from the Indian subcontinent with modern techniques and styles.

Keith is the author of three other books, *The Perfect Turkey, The Farmers Dinner Cookbook,* and *Meat: The Ultimate Cookbook*. For more on Keith and his work, follow him on Instagram (@keithsarasin) or visit him at his website, keithsarasin.com.

ABOUT CIDER MILL PRESS BOOK PUBLISHERS

Good ideas ripen with time. From seed to harvest, Cider Mill Press brings fine reading, information, and entertainment together between the covers of its creatively crafted books. Our Cider Mill bears fruit twice a year, publishing a new crop of titles each spring and fall.

"Where Good Books Are Ready for Press"

501 Nelson Place
Nashville, Tennessee 37214

cidermillpress.com